W9-DEF-275

EDITH STEIN

by Arthur Giron

Parkway Central High Theatre
369 N. Woods Mill Road
Chesterfield, MO 63017

S A M U E L   F R E N C H ,   I N C .

45 WEST 25TH STREET   NEW YORK 10010
7623 SUNSET BOULEVARD   HOLLYWOOD 90046
LONDON   *TORONTO*

Copyright © 1988, 1991 by Arthur Giron

ALL RIGHTS RESERVED

CAUTION: Professionals and amateurs are hereby warned that EDITH STEIN is subject to a royalty. It is fully protected under the copyright laws of the United States of America, the British Commonwealth, including Canada, and all other countries of the Copyright Union. All rights, including professional, amateur, motion pictures, recitation, lecturing, public reading, radio broadcasting, television, and the rights of translation into foreign languages are strictly reserved. In its present form the play is dedicated to the reading public only.

The amateur live stage performance rights to EDITH STEIN are controlled exclusively by Samuel French, Inc., and royalty arrangements and licenses must be secured well in advance of presentation. PLEASE NOTE that amateur royalty fees are set upon application in accordance with your producing circumstances. When applying for a royalty quotation and license please give us the number of performances intended, dates of production, your seating capacity and admission fee. Royalties are payable one week before the opening performance of the play to Samuel French, Inc., at 45 West 25th Street, New York, NY 10010-2751; or at 7623 Sunset Blvd., Hollywood, CA 90046-2795, or to Samuel French (Canada), Ltd., 100 Lombard Street, Toronto, Ontario, Canada M5C 1M3.

Royalty of the required amount must be paid whether the play is presented for charity or gain and whether or not admission is charged.

Stock royalty quoted on application to Samuel French, Inc.

For all other rights than those stipulated above, apply to Barbara Hogenson Agency, 19 West 44th Street, Suite 1000, NY, NY 10036.

Particular emphasis is laid on the question of amateur or professional readings, permission and terms for which must be secured in writing from Samuel French, Inc.

Copying from this book in whole or in part is strictly forbidden by law, and the right of performance is not transferable.

Whenever the play is produced the following notice must appear on all programs, printing and advertising for the play: "Produced by special arrangement with Samuel French, Inc."

Due authorship credit must be given on all programs, printing and advertising for the play.

ISBN 0 573 69248 3   Printed in U.S.A.

No one shall commit or authorize any act or omission by which the copyright of, or the right to copyright, this play may be impaired.

No one shall make any changes in this play for the purpose of production.

Publication of this play does not imply availability for performance. Both amateurs and professionals considering a production are *strongly* advised in their own interests to apply to Samuel French, Inc., for written permission before starting rehearsals, advertising, or booking a theatre.

No part of this book may be reproduced, stored in a retrieval system, or transmitted in any form, by any means, now known or yet to be invented, including mechanical, electronic, photocopying, recording, videotaping, or otherwise, without the prior written permission of the publisher.

IMPORTANT BILLING AND CREDIT REQUIREMENTS

All producers of EDITH STEIN *must* give credit to the Author of the Play in all programs distributed in connection with performances of the Play and in all instances in which the title of the Play appears for purposes of advertising, publicizing or otherwise exploiting the Play and/or a production. The name of the Author *must* also appear on a separate line, on which no other name appears, immediately following the title, and *must* appear in size of type not less than fifty percent the size of the title type.

Edith Stein was produced by the Pittsburgh Public Theater in January, 1988. It was directed by Lee Sankowich and had the following cast:

WEISMANN	Anthony Mainionis
PRIORESS	Susan Riskin
EDITH STEIN	Helena Ruoti
STEFAN	David Yezzi
FRAU STEIN	Lynne Charnay
HANNAH REINACH	Maura Minteer
KARL-HEINZ	Jim Abele
BERNHARDT	Jens Krummel
SISTER RUTH	Kate English
SISTER PRUDENCE	Nann Mogg
FARMER, NAZI SOLDIER	Wynn Harmon
NAZI SOLDIER	William Salzmann

CHARACTERS

EDITH STEIN
FRAU STEIN, Edith's mother
CLARA, Edith's niece
HANNAH REINACH

DR. SAUL WEISMAN

THE PRIORESS
SISTER PRUDENCE
SISTER RUTH

KARL-HEINZ
FRANZY
BERNHARDT, a Nazi soldier

The play takes place in the Carmelite convent outside the gates of Auschwitz in 1987. Simultaneously, we travel to various locations throughout Germany during the years following the First World War to 1942.

This play was inspired by Edith Stein. It is not a documentary depiction of her life, but an attempt to dramatize the conflicts she faced. Nevertheless, every care has been taken to select key moments in her life and to fathom her essential nature in theatrical terms. This has necessitated the severe compression of time and the addition of fictional characters to complement the important persons who actually interacted with her.

Edith always said she loved the theatre. She, herself, wrote skits for family celebrations and performed in them. Even in the convent she continued to write short plays, and we are told, wore a red wig over her nun's headdress while acting in a convent play. We follow her into the theater now.

PROLOGUE

Terrifying SOUNDS: marching Nazi soldiers, trains transporting human cargo. Quickly, this noise is replaced by the voices of WOMEN singing a sublime, ancient song. In the distance, we begin to see TWO NUNS standing perfectly still. This is the Carmelite convent outside the gates of Auschwitz. It is 1987. DR. SAUL WEISMANN enters the parlor, carrying a briefcase. HE listens to the nuns CHANTING, then extends his hand into the air and pulls down on an imaginary bell cord hanging from the ceiling. The parlor BELL resounds through the old brick building, formerly a theater during the Austro-Hungarian Empire. THE PRIORESS appears. She is separated from Dr. Weismann by an imaginary grille.

PRIORESS. Come closer. Are you hungry? Are you thirsty? Are you in need of prayers? May we help you in any way?

WEISMANN. I represent the International Holocaust Committee.

PRIORESS. Ah, yes, Dr. Weismann. We've been expecting you. May we offer you something cool to refresh you after your long journey?

WEISMANN. No, thank you. Reverend Mother, do you know the pain you are causing? I speak for Jews around the world. To establish a convent here is—!

PRIORESS. Tell me what I need to hear. I am not made of sugar.

WEISMANN. The presence of the Cross at the gates of Auschwitz is an outrage.

PRIORESS. We are here to bear the weight of the Cross.

WEISMANN. It is indeed heavy, Reverend Mother. We have felt the weight of it for centuries. Who has killed us if not you?

PRIORESS. It is up to Christians to expiate the evil perpetrated by other Christians. False Christians. Nazi pagans.

WEISMANN. And so you appropriate the Holocaust as your own.

PRIORESS. Must you have the exclusive right to sorrow?

WEISMANN. I know many others died here. But is this camp particularly central to the identity of non-Jews? Jews are Jews because we share the anguish suffered here. It is part of our collective experience. Don't displace us. Your convent must be closed. The name of Edith Stein must not be glorified in Auschwitz. To name a community of nuns after a convert leads many to believe that what you are doing is praying for the conversion of all Jews.

PRIORESS. No, no she would never have wanted to offend her own in any way. No.

WEISMANN. Then remove her name from this community immediately.

PRIORESS. That would be like killing her a second time ...

WEISMANN. So many were martyred here, yet the Pope has raised her to the rank of Blessed. Was beatified. The last step before sainthood. Why? Have we returned to medieval times? Is the Church sending me a message that it wants my soul, too?

PRIORESS. Dr. Weismann, would you like some strong liquor? We always have a bottle of Christmas juice handy for emergencies.

WEISMANN. No, thank you.

PRIORESS. Then, later, I would be honored if you would sit at our table and break bread with us.

WEISMANN. You are very gracious, but I am certain that our business will be concluded before the dinner hour.

PRIORESS. Sir, I pray we can arrive at a compromise.

WEISMANN. No compromise is possible where the memory of our dead is concerned. Our past is our future. And I am here to protect it.

PRIORESS. Yes, Dr. Weismann. Memories are sacred. And we must do everything to protect them.

(EDITH STEIN appears. SHE lights a cigarette. SHE carries a pen and the manuscript of her family history. WEISMANN sees her immediately. At this point, THE PRIORESS does not.)

WEISMANN. You knew her?

PRIORESS. Sister Teresa Benedicta of the Cross, in the world Edith Stein. I knew her very well.

WEISMANN. Did she smoke?

PRIORESS. Never!

EDITH. I don't know what I'd do without my cigarettes and black coffee.

WEISMANN. Why did she convert?

PRIORESS. No one knows. She kept that a secret. But I do know that she was deeply affected by nursing the troops during the first world war.

Scene 1

[NOTE: Although the play is divided into scenes, the play never stops flowing continuously.]
We are now in Edith's home in Breslau. The first world war has just ended. The PRIORESS and DR.

WEISMANN begin to disappear from view as EDITH writes in her manuscript.

EDITH. I don't know what I'd do without my home, my family and the festival of Purim!

(A burst of LIGHT, COLOR and MUSIC. The stage fills with merrymakers—ACTORS who will play other roles later, but who will be unrecognizable because now THEY are wearing masks and homemade costumes.)

ALL SING:
"OH, ONCE THERE WAS A WICKED MAN,[*]
AND HAMAN WAS HIS NAME, SIR.
HE WOULD HAVE MURDERED ALL THE JEWS,
THO' THEY WERE NOT TO BLAME, SIR."

"OH, TODAY WE'LL MERRY, MERRY BE,
OH, TODAY WE'LL MERRY, MERRY BE,
AND 'NASH SOME HOMENTASHEN!"

THE PLAY! THE PLAY! THE PURIM PLAY!

(EVERYONE sits on the floor in a semi-circle. EDITH runs about making preparations for the play—handing out noisemakers, pieces of chalk, scripts, etc.)

FRAU STEIN. Who has been dropping Homentashen on the floor? No, I will never have another Purim party if you children don't learn to eat properly! And look—Little Clara with a runny nose! (*Gives her a handkerchief.*) Blow, darling. Where is your mother? Purim this year is a

---

[*] "A Wicked Man" by Miriam Meyers, in *The Jewish Songster*, I. and S.F. Goldfarb, Brooklyn, New York.

disaster—everyone is drunk and dropping their cookies...!
Well, good night. I am going to bed.

(Cries of protest from ALL.)

FRAU STEIN. No. No play. You are not real Jews. I
don't want to have anything to do with you modern
children. No. No play tonight.

WOMAN. Mama, we haven't had a Purim play since
before the war.

MAN. The first thing Edith did when she got back from
the front was to write a Purim play for tonight.

CLARA. What's a Purim play?

FRAU STEIN. When I am dead, who in this house will
see to it that our beautiful Jewish traditions are kept alive?
My darling doctors and scholars and scientists, which one
of you will take the responsibility of gathering the family
together to celebrate the High Holy Days? Who? Not one
of you?

MAN. Oh, Mama, don't be so glum. We want to
celebrate the Armistice.

ALL. The play! The play! We want the play! The play!
The play! We want the play!

FRAU STEIN. Well ... Just for the children, so they
will learn. Quickly before the little ones get sleepy.

(ALL cheer.)

EDITH. Did you all use the chalk to write the name of
wicked Haman on the soles of your shoes? Now, every
time the name of wicked Haman is said stomp your feet
hard on the floor and use your groggers[*] to obliterate that
evil name forever! Children, Grandma says Purim is so

---

[*] noisemakers

important for us because it celebrates how Esther saved the children of Israel from destruction.

FRAU STEIN. A woman did that. A woman can do anything. Look at me, left a widow with seven children. I saved you all from destruction—

(GROANS, Ad lib "Oh, Mama...", "Here she goes again...")

EDITH. Where is Franzy?

(A handsome, Germanic youth steps forward. HE hasn't pulled on his mask yet.)

FRANZY. Here!
EDITH. Come here, sweetie. Now all of you, Franzy has been nice enough to volunteer to portray the proud villain, Haman. This boy is our Christian neighbor who doesn't know our traditions, so don't spank him too hard at the end of the play.

(EDITH pulls on his mask, pushes FRANZY center stage, and blows on a toy trumpet to announce the start of the play.)

HAMAN. I am Haman!

(BOOS, STOMPING, NOISEMAKERS.)

FRAU STEIN. Pride cometh before a fall.
HAMAN. Bow to me. Everyone bows down when I pass.

(MORDECAI enters wearing a long false beard.)

HAMAN. *You.* Old man. Bow down before me.
MORDECAI. No.
HAMAN. What?!
MORDECAI. No.
HAMAN. What?!
MORDECAI. No.
HAMAN. Who are you?
MORDECAI. I am Mordecai. A nice Jewish man.

(APPLAUSE.)

HAMAN. And I am Haman.

(NOISE.)

HAMAN. Old man, why do you not bow before me?
MORDECAI. No disrespect, Sir. But I bow before no one but God—for I AM A JEW!

(APPLAUSE.)

HAMAN. Then I will have all the Jews in Prussia killed.
EDITH. Persia not Prussia.

(FRANZY is momentarily confused.)

EDITH. THIS is Prussia.
HAMAN. Then I will have all the Jews in ... Prussia killed.

(EDITH throws up her hands.)

HAMAN. And I will get the Kaiser's permission to do it, too.

CLARA. Ha. Haman. The Kaiser is married to Esther. A Jew.

HAMAN. Queen Esther, who lives in the castle, is a Jew? I didn't know that.

ALL. (*Ad lib.*) Shhhhh. Quiet, Clara. Don't tell ...

FRAU STEIN. Clara, come over and sit by Grandma. And while we finish watching the play you help me to fill these baskets for the poor people in the neighborhood. You know, it's a very important part of Purim to later go out into the street and give nice things to those who are not as fortunate as we.

HAMAN. I am proud Haman.

(NOISE.)

HAMAN. The King respects me. I have his ear.

(EDITH hands him a large, cardboard ear.)

KING. Who has got my ear?

HAMAN. I do. So listen. There's a bad foreign element in the land. Jews. They should be wiped out.

KING. Why do you want to kill all the Jews in Persia?

HAMAN. The Jews won't bow. Can I kill them?

KING. It is decreed.

HAMAN. Good!

(HE stomps around to "boos.")

ALL. Esther! Esther! Esther! Esther!

FRAU STEIN. Edith! Edith!

EDITH. No! Erna is more beautiful ...

FRAU STEIN: Erna will do it next year. Edith, you are more woman than you know. You were born for great things. (*To the Others.*) The Kaiser gave her a medal for her good nursing in the war.

WOMAN. Edith wrote the play, she can't be in it! Erna should do it.

FRAU STEIN. Edith can do anything. She is *my* Esther. (*To Edith.*) Be our Esther.

(EDITH turns away.)

FRAU STEIN. Children, Edith is in trouble. She can't get work. She spends all day in the attic smoking, alone, confused, smoking, thinking too much. She is in shock. The war ... encountering death every day ... they brought her bodies from the battlefield to bathe ... Last week, when she walked me to Temple, Edith stepped right into the traffic. A trolley almost ran her over. I don't know where her mind is, I don't know what is to become of her. I am going crazy.

Nothing pleases her: before the war she goes off to study psychology, I say fine. She says not fine. She gives up studying psychology because she says it is an inexact science. She is looking for answers, she says. So, she says she is going to study philosophy. Fine. The day Edith becomes a Doctor of Philosophy she tells me with a laurel crown on her head, a scholar's crown—I am so happy that day and she tells me it is the emptiest day of her life!

(EDITH puts a cigarette in her mouth. FRAU STEIN yanks it out of her mouth and hurls it to the floor.)

FRAU STEIN. A cigarette is a poor substitute for God, Edith! If you believed, had faith, you wouldn't be so lost. It is my fault. I didn't see to it that any of you had a sound religious education. You boys at least had a little Hebrew. But you girls—nothing. It is my fault you are all agnostics, atheists, and unbelievers. And God will punish me for it, I know. I am sorry, children. If your father had lived ... (*SHE goes to Edith.*) If your father were here, alive, he would want you to feel like a queen tonight. Be our queen ... (*SHE drapes a beautiful, diaphanous scarf over Edith's head. SHE then lays a gold laurel crown on Edith's head.*) Esther has been praying and fasting for three days to find the courage to go before the King. Find the courage.

(EDITH, as ESTHER, moves toward the KING.)

KING. Esther, my bride, what do you want?
EDITH. (*Kneels before him.*) My Lord, if I have found favor with you, I ask that you spare the lives of my people.
KING. Your people?
EDITH. I am a Jew.

(Beat. HE raises her up lovingly.)

KING. Brave woman, I grant your prayer.
FRAU STEIN. And the Lord saved His people from destruction.

(THE GROUP applauds. LIGHTS begin to change. As the lights dim to a magical blue, so the SOUND dims. Applauding hands come together, but we hear no sound. In slow motion, the partygoers dance off as in the distance VOICES sing. "Oh, today we'll merry, merry be, Oh, today we'll merry, merry be ..." EDITH and FRAU STEIN are left alone.)

EDITH. Mama, I'll clean everything. You go to bed.
FRAU STEIN. I don't want to go to bed.

EDITH. I'll put on the record of "The Beautiful Blue Danube Waltz." It always helps you to fall asleep.

FRAU STEIN. Talk to me, Edith.

EDITH. I have no one else to talk with, that's true.

FRAU STEIN. Then talk.

EDITH. I am wrestling with death, Mama.

FRAU STEIN. It's not polite to talk about death. You talk about death too much. No, we do not speak of death in this house.

EDITH. Mama, do you believe that some day you will be reunited with Papa ... in eternity ...?

FRAU STEIN. Silence! Be silent, child. What cannot be understood is forbidden.

EDITH. Mama, word came that Professor Reinach was killed in the war. What his wife must be suffering. I must go to her. But what am I to tell her? How can I console her?

FRAU STEIN. I will bake a Challah for Hannah Reinach.

EDITH. Console me, Mama!

FRAU STEIN. Put on the record of "The Beautiful Blue Danube." I want to dance with my daughter before she goes away from me again.

(EDITH puts the record on the Victrola, cranks it up. THEY dance. Then, EDITH picks up a suitcase, starts to leave, turns to FRAU STEIN, who blows her a kiss. Crossfade.)

Scene 2

HANNAH. Edith! Edith! Stop dreaming and start climbing!

(HANNAH REINACH is discovered sitting in an apple tree.)

EDITH. Frau Reinach ...?

HANNAH. Up here in the tree!

EDITH. I thought you said we were going to pick apples?

HANNAH. How do you pick apples?

EDITH. I don't know?

HANNAH. Climb! Without your shoes and stockings, that's how.

EDITH. Frau Reinach can't we keep walking? We haven't had a minute to talk seriously since I got off the train.

HANNAH. Oh, it's glorious up here! Don't you want to see the university?

EDITH. Yes. Yes.

HANNAH. I have a perfect view of the bell tower.

(In the distance, the university BELL starts ringing.)

HANNAH. Oh, do you hear that? Calling the students to class.

EDITH. I'm coming. I'm coming, Frau Reinach. (*SHE quickly takes off shoes, stockings.*)

HANNAH. (Sings)
The Tree of Life my soul has seen,
Laden with fruit and always green."*

EDITH. This is the strangest condolence call I've ever made.

HANNAH.
"The Tree of Life my soul has seen,

---

* Composer unknown. An old English folk ballad. Can be omitted.

Laden with fruit and always green."

Hurry! Hurry!

EDITH. (*Starts climbing. This sort of activity is difficult for her.*) I'm coming, Frau Reinach.

HANNAH. You don't have to be formal with me. Call me, Hannah.

EDITH. Yes, Hannah. Ouch!

HANNAH. I'm not sending you home until your legs are scratched up and down from climbing fruit trees.

(EDITH is reaching the top.)

HANNAH. It's the best cure, I found. A good climb, barefoot, in the open air—ahh. The best thing for the soul is to be in the sun, sitting high up where we can see all the good things God created for us. See—the cornfields, and the river, the old town, and the great university that meant so much to us.

EDITH. How beautiful. I miss all this so much. I long to be part of a community again. Oh! I'm going to fall!

HANNAH. Don't. There's a branch with apples right behind you. Stretch! And when we're finished gathering apples here, we shall go to a pear orchard, then an apricot orchard. Now, hurry up before we're discovered!

EDITH. What? You mean we don't have permission to pick apples here?

HANNAH. Darling, it's much better for the circulation NOT to have permission.

FARMER. (*Off.*) Get down from there you two!

EDITH. The farmer heard you!

HANNAH. Come down! Hurry up! Don't drop any apples!

(Laughing, THEY scurry down from the trees, trying not to drop apples. THEY run.)

HANNAH. This way.
EDITH. What about my shoes?
HANNAH. Forget 'em.
FARMER. *(Off.)* Stop! Thieves!

(THE YOUNG WOMEN yell back from a hidden position.)

HANNAH. Keep our shoes. Pre-war. Worth more than your rotten apples!
EDITH. Your apples have worms. *(SHE starts out.)*
HANNAH. No! This way! I know where we can steal some blueberries on the way home.

(THEY rush off.)

FARMER. *(Off.)* Disrespectful kids, criminals! Communists! Anarchists! Heathens! Jews! Students!

(THE PRIORESS and DR. WEISMANN enter. SHE carries a wooden box.)

PRIORESS. This is my Edith box. During the Second World War our convent was destroyed. But I was given permission to search the rubble for whatever I could find that belonged to her—*(SHE opens the box, begins to take out items.)*—a postcard, some photographs of her nieces and nephews, and the family history she was writing and never finished because she was arrested. *(SHE hands Weismann the manuscript of Edith's family history.)*

(THE YOUNG WOMEN rush on with apples in their skirts. THEY fall laughing, exhausted beside an imaginary stream.)

EDITH. My feet are killing me!

WEISMANN. This Professor Reinach and his wife were Jewish?

PRIORESS. Yes.

WEISMANN. But, they became Christians?

PRIORESS. Well ... Lutherans.

WEISMANN. Oh.

PRIORESS. This young couple was a whole new world to her.

EDITH. I loved him.

HANNAH. You made him happy in ways I never could. And I am grateful to you. He said you surpassed him in knowledge.

EDITH. But where is my knowledge now? I have no knowledge. I came here to console you, and I don't have one word of comfort for you. In all my reading, I have not found any concrete proof that any of us can triumph over death. *(SHE opens her suitcase.)* It is the central problem of our lives, how do we keep the people we love alive?

(THE PRIORESS and DR. WEISMANN begin to disappear.)

EDITH. My mother baked you this Challah.

HANNAH. Oh! *(SHE takes the beautiful, braided bread in HER hands, holding it with great care—almost awe. It is very precious to her. HANNAH breathes in the smell of the bread.)*

HANNAH. I am not alone in the world! Edith, you are the only person who has come to visit me since my husband was killed. I love Challah! I will make us some hot chocolate and you can taste my apple marmalade.

EDITH. No one from your families has come?

HANNAH. Oh, we have been dead to our families for years.

EDITH. But almost all the Jewish professors became Christians to keep their teaching positions. Don't your people see that?

HANNAH. I adore Challah. I haven't had any in so long. Do you mind—?

(SHE begins to eat ravenously, offers Edith some. But EDITH only takes a morsel.)

EDITH. Tell me how he died.

HANNAH. He was fighting in the trenches in Flanders. He drowned in the mud, covered by a blanket of rats.

EDITH. The bodies of the soldiers I bathed were covered with rat bites, mud, lice. Blood stuck their clothing to their skin. The uniforms had to be burned: many had cholera, typhoid, contagious diseases. Only a handful of us wanted to get near them.

HANNAH. The war has not ended here. Everyone is a little insane these days with grief. Bands of unemployed young boys have slaughtered entire herds with butcher knives, as if the cattle were British soldiers. They cannot abide the loss of pride we must endure. Healthy young men have been transformed by the despair of defeat.

EDITH. It horrifies me to think that we're going to have a generation of uneducated men roaming about in years to come. So many teachers have died. The classrooms are empty. And still I cannot get a teaching position.

HANNAH. But with your credentials—!

EDITH. That's why I haven't come sooner. I applied to every university in Germany. Everywhere men in grey beards addressed me contemptuously as "The Philosopher Lady."

HANNAH. If you are rejected by those men, turn to academic women. There's a forward-thinking teachers college, not far, run by Dominican nuns.

EDITH. How can nuns be forward-thinking?

HANNAH. May I write to them on your behalf? It's a beautiful community of selfless, educated, kind women, who believe in the unique abilities of women to alter the course of German history for the better. And in the meantime, *I* will give you work. You can help me put my husband's papers in order! Prepare all his thoughts for publication! And we can climb apple trees, take walks. Edith, you are going to rest your mind—for the first time in your life. We're going to have a lovely time. I'm so happy.

EDITH. You have outdone me in courage.

HANNAH. I am content.

EDITH. How can you be? Why aren't you dressed all in black, in deepest despair...? I don't understand it.

HANNAH. He just got there ahead of me, that's all.

EDITH. Where?

HANNAH. Paradise.

EDITH. How can you believe that?!

HANNAH. I feel his presence very strongly. (*Beat.*) You're getting too much sun. You're not used to it. (*Tries to take Edith's hand.*) Come on, let's go into the church across the road. It's dark and cool in there.

EDITH. No.

HANNAH. That's what it's for, to get in out of the heat or the cold.

EDITH. I shouldn't have come ...

HANNAH. Don't be afraid. There's nobody in there. Please, Edith. You don't look well. This church is of considerable historical interest.

EDITH. Can I smoke in there?
HANNAH. Of course.

(THEY take a few steps upstage. The LIGHTS dim and THEY are in the church.*)

EDITH. It's so quiet. We're going to be thrown out.

(An OLD PEASANT WOMAN** enters carrying a basket. Bathed in the reflection of a stained glass window, SHE sets the basket down, kneels and begins praying, head bowed.)

EDITH. What's she doing?
HANNAH. She is praying.
EDITH. Is there going to be a service here soon?
HANNAH. No.
EDITH. You mean she can come in here and pray any time she wants to?
HANNAH. Yes. I have a present for you. It was my husband's last postcard to me. (*SHE takes a postcard out of her apron pocket, and reads.*) "The first weeks were frightening. Then God's peace came to me. Now all is well."

(SHE hands it to EDITH, who hesitates taking it.)

HANNAH. Please.

(EDITH takes it.)

---

* In the Pittsburgh Public Theater production, the sound designer turned on a microphone at this point that gave the women's voices an echo resonance.
** Played by the actress who plays SISTER PRUDENCE.

HANNAH. The Cross was a great comfort to him.

EDITH. Professor Reinach is not in paradise. He is here... with us.

(Crossfade to:)

Scene 3

A prison chapel. CHRIST appears, entering from the back, strides to a strong position center stage. As the LIGHTING becomes brighter, we begin to realize that this impressive vision is KARL-HEINZ, wearing a flowing, white muslin robe; a wig of long, beautiful, brown hair; a matching false beard; and a crown of thorns. Obviously, KARL-HEINZ has taken a great deal of trouble to assemble this costume, and to alter his appearance. The effect is uncanny, disturbing. HE speaks in a powerful, pleasing voice.

KARL-HEINZ. "Whoever seeks to save his *life* will *lose* it. And whoever loses his life will preserve it." (*HE tries to improve his delivery as an actor would.*) "Whoever *seeks* to *save* his life will lose it." (*Romantically.*) Look at me, ladies. Lean out on your windowsills, lean your creamy breasts way out, behold The Way of the Cross.

(FRANZY, now a grown-up young man in a leather jacket, steps out of the shadows and watches Karl-Heinz.)

KARL-HEINZ. A kiss of peace is all I want, a kiss. Marry me, and we'll produce a son who'll be a giant among men. A Savior!

FRANZY. Women always love men they can't have ...

KARL-HEINZ. What?

FRANZY. Men behind bars.

KARL-HEINZ. Get the hell out of here.

FRANZY. And Holy Men.

KARL-HEINZ. I have permission to practice in here. The prison chapel is mine. Get out!

FRANZY. *I* am a Holy Man of sorts. I work for the Ministry of Church Affairs, Karl-Heinz. I'm only a beginner, but already doors open to me, legs ... Your religious festivals here in the prison have become quite famous. And tomorrow! It's going to be quite an event: prisoners allowed to leave their cells to perform a Passion Play outside the prison walls in the village square! My congratulations. You have brilliant powers of persuasion.

KARL-HEINZ. Have you got a mirror, a pocket mirror? They don't give us mirrors here. Even for shaving.

(FRANZY laughs and hands KARL-HEINZ a pocket mirror. KARL-HEINZ studies himself proudly.)

KARL-HEINZ. I got permission for my men to be released *two* days, not just one.

FRANZY. I know. I saw your fellow inmates working in the street spreading pine on the cobblestones.

KARL-HEINZ. For me and my cross to walk on.

FRANZY. It's not the same as being led through the streets with a humiliating placard hanging from your neck announcing that you had broken the racial laws. What did it say? "I am a swine, I made a Jewess Mine"?

KARL-HEINZ. No, it just said, "I took a Jewess to my room." My landlady reported me because I owed her back rent.

FRANZY. Was she beautiful?

KARL-HEINZ. I'd say she was the most attractive landlady I ever had. *I* never pay rent.

FRANZY. The Jewess. Was *she* worth this humiliation?

KARL-HEINZ. A waitress.

FRANZY. You don't pay for your meals either?

KARL-HEINZ. I don't pay for anything.

FRANZY. Just a stiff prison sentence for taking your pleasure with a Jewish woman.

KARL-HEINZ. I didn't know that she was. Do you think I would knowingly couple my body with one of those Christ-killers? Believe me I have scrubbed myself raw to remove all trace of her flesh. I love my body. Speaking man to man, I have a big soul.

FRANZY. Congratulations.

KARL-HEINZ. From now on I'm not going to waste myself rutting like some mountain goat. I'm more god than goat. And I plan to find a goddess to receive my celestial seed.

FRANZY. My superiors will be relieved to learn that you have purified yourself.

KARL-HEINZ. Know any nice Aryan goddesses— who'll wait for me?

FRANZY. Ah we're all big souls seeking expression. Aren't we? Karl-Heinz, you've done enough penance. I have your release. ...

(HE shows Karl-Heinz a sheet of official paper. KARL-HEINZ tries to take it.)

FRANZY. Wait. If you get out, you come to work for us.

KARL-HEINZ. Are you S.S.?

FRANZY. A special branch. Under the mantle of the Ministry of Church Affairs. Right now we are recruiting a select class of men—visionaries who want to elevate the populace onto a higher, spiritual plain. You would be one of the founders of a new religion—The National Reich Church of Germany. But first there is a lot of house cleaning to do—Jews, Catholics, Freemasons. And it will take you years of hard work and discipline before you are eligible to take the official oath of our fellowship.

KARL-HEINZ. I don't think so.

FRANZY. Why not?

KARL-HEINZ. How many times in a man's life does he get a chance to be Jesus Christ?

FRANZY. You can have your glory tomorrow.

KARL-HEINZ. Can I keep your mirror?

FRANZY. Yes.

KARL-HEINZ. All right. I'll be one of your Holy Men.

FRANZY. Not so easy. First you must show us what you are made of. Tomorrow at the climax of the Passion you must find some way to discredit Christ.

KARL-HEINZ. How?

FRANZY. We will be watching. If you succeed, you will join the ranks of a new order of men—no longer allied to effeminate foreign churches—(*HE puts a swastika arm band on Karl-Heinz's arm.*)—but who claim kinship with giants, the true Germanic gods of old. (*HE leaves.*)

KARL-HEINZ. (*Looks at himself in the mirror.*) You are a giant. A god!

(*Crossfade to:*)

Scene 4

CLARA enters singing. Since we saw her ten years ago, SHE has become an adolescent. EDITH enters from the opposite side of the stage carrying her small suitcase. SHE wears a conservative suit, a hat, and gloves.

CLARA.
"Oh, today we'll merry, merry be,
Oh, today we'll merry, merry be ..."

(When EDITH sees her, SHE starts singing, too.)

EDITH.
"Oh, today we'll merry, merry be,"
   BOTH.
"And 'nash some Homentashen!"
   EDITH. Clara...?!
   CLARA. Tante Edith...?!
   EDITH. Clara, darling.

(THEY give each other a big hug. EDITH kneels, opens her suitcase)

EDITH. I've brought you a box of paints.
CLARA. Where'd you get it? Jews can't shop at the art store any more. Oh, I forgot. Papa said you'd become a Christian all of a sudden.
EDITH. I became a Christian ten years ago. Before I began teaching with the Dominican nuns. Not now.
CLARA. Papa told us last week.
EDITH. I wanted to tell you when it happened, after the war. But Grandma didn't want the little ones to know.
CLARA. You should have said.
EDITH. Yes. I should have said. I'm sorry.

(Beat. CLARA throws her arms around her aunt's neck.)

CLARA. I'm so glad your home now.
EDITH. Clara, I want to tell you something. I've been dismissed from my teaching position because I am a Jew.

But I'm applying for a new position, a whole new life. If I'm accepted it means I'll have to go away again.

CLARA. You're on the side of the bad people now, the ones who are hurting the lumber business.

EDITH. Clara! What about the lumber business?

CLARA. Nobody's buying from us anymore.

EDITH. Mama didn't say ... Clara, listen to me, dear. A great painter, Clara, probably spends a great deal of her time painting. I need to spend a great deal of my time praying. Darling, I've discovered that I have the power of prayer in me. You remember, a long time ago when we did the play of Esther on the Festival of Purim?

CLARA. Sure, I'd like to be like her.

EDITH. Me, too. You remember that Esther had to leave her people to go live with the King in his castle? And once she was inside she was able to get the King's ear. You remember that ear?

(THEY chuckle.)

CLARA. I remember.

EDITH. See, that's what I want to do. Get God's ear. Implore Him to save our people from destruction. I'm going to be praying for your well being day and night. I'm not really leaving you behind. No. I will never separate from you in my heart.

CLARA. We're thinking about packing up and going away, too.

EDITH. Where?

CLARA. To America.

EDITH. America! I had an article published in a small magazine printed in America. The magazine is edited in a place called Buffalo. The editors invited me to go to Buffalo to lecture there.

CLARA. Good! Where is Buffalo?

EDITH. I don't know. We could look it up on a map.

CLARA. All right.

EDITH. Clara, maybe someday we'll all be happy together again. In Buffalo.

(CLARA runs out. EDITH kneels behind her suitcase.)

EDITH. Oh, dear Lord, the greatest pain we will ever know, I am told, is suffered when the soul is ripped from the body at the moment of death. My mother will experience such anguish if I leave her side to enter the religious life. I love her. But, Lord, I have the will to reverse history. The Cross falls on my people—please, I want to bear their pains in my body. Please, Lord, bring justice to this land. Justice. Justice! JUSTICE! *(SHE collapses weeping.)* Mercy, mercy, mercy ... *(EDITH collects herself, gets up, picks up her suitcase, and steps into the next scene. Crossfade:)*

Scene 5

A Carmelite convent. NUNS chant. The stage is empty as EDITH enters the parlor. EDITH sets her suitcase down. SHE listens to the chanting for a moment. It renews her strength. SHE extends her hand into the air and pulls down on an imaginary bell cord hanging from the ceiling. The BELL rings. THE PRIORESS enters with forceful energy followed by a lovely young nun, SISTER RUTH, and an ageless, beautiful, older nun, SISTER PRUDENCE. THEY group themselves near the imaginary grille that separates the interior of the convent from the parlor. In reality, a Carmelite convent grille—which can be very large or very small—is an opaque screen, covered by a black curtain, somewhat

*like the grille in a confessional. Since Carmelites are a
cloistered order—rarely does a nun come out once she is
admitted—the grille is their only "window" with the
outside world. SISTER RUTH carries a small stool for
SISTER PRUDENCE, who has brought her sewing.*

PRIORESS. Dr . Stein?

EDITH. Yes?

PRIORESS. Dr. Stein, the Bishop has spoken to us
about you.

EDITH. Please pull back the curtain. It unnerves me so.

PRIORESS. We have a strict vow of enclosure.

EDITH. Don't you want to see me? I want to see you.

PRIORESS. Dr. Stein, we are an extreme order. We do
not teach or nurse. Our mother Teresa of Avila followed
the example of your forefather Elijah, who fasted and
sought solitude in the desert. My cell is like a hermit's
cave. It is a life of prayer only, of discipline, mortification.
You must have a great love to take up your Cross every
day. Only such a love can make the life possible. It is one
of all or nothing. It is a battleground!

EDITH. Halfway measures do not satisfy me.

PRIORESS. Dr. Stein ... my, this is the first time
we've had an applicant who was a Doctor of Philosophy ...
Dr. Stein, it would be sinful for you to give up your
intellectual labors. Our library—

EDITH—I've read too much.

PRIORESS. Let me urge you to go elsewhere.

EDITH. Reverend Mother, I have the appropriate
credentials. I am a healthy woman. I come from a loving
family. My heart vibrates with the prayers of my
forefathers—the Psalms of David, the Songs of Solomon,
the Lamentations of Jeremiah. The Magnificat, which
sprang from the overflowing heart of the Virgin. I desire to
join my voice to those prayers, transmitted from mouth to

mouth, from generation to generation. It is a share in Christ's passion that I desire. Reverend Mother, I have the appropriate credentials!

PRIORESS. Whether you are admitted or not will depend on the vote of every sister in this community. There are many applicants. Perhaps you will be chosen— perhaps not. Sometimes our prayers are not answered in the way we think they should be. Do you understand?

EDITH. Yes, Reverend Mother.

PRIORESS. What was that?

EDITH. I said, "Yes, Reverend Mother."

PRIORESS. You'll have to speak loudly and clearly. Although some of us are quite young, some of us ... (*SHE looks at Sister Prudence.*) ... are reaching that blessed state known as senility. ...

PRUDENCE. Hrumph.

PRIORESS. ... and are, therefore, hard of hearing. I don't know why it is, but Carmelites are known for their longevity.

EDITH. Could sleeping in your coffins have anything to do with it?

PRIORESS. What?

EDITH. I was only joking. People have so many misconceptions about the Carmelites.

PRIORESS. Yes.

EDITH. I've heard many tongues tell that each of you has a skull in her cell to remind you that death comes to all of us.

PRIORESS. It is not true that we sleep in coffins. However, we recently received a particularly fine skull from a policeman that will grace my table at mealtimes.

EDITH. Between the salt and the pepper?

PRIORESS. I beg your pardon?

EDITH. I was just trying to picture it.

PRUDENCE. What did she say?

EDITH. You all must have very strong stomachs. That's probably why you live so long.

PRUDENCE. I haven't chewed on a piece of red meat for fifty years ...

PRIORESS. Sister Prudence ...

PRUDENCE. Do you like fish?

EDITH. I love fish.

PRUDENCE. My dear, could you eat it three-hundred and sixty-five days a year?

EDITH. Yes, Sister Prudence.

PRUDENCE. A wise girl. Meat is the ruination of mankind.

PRIORESS. Sister Prudence

PRUDENCE. We're surrounded by flesh eaters!

PRIORESS. We must go on.

PRUDENCE. A nation of flesh eaters!

PRIORESS. Please answer our questions briefly. When were you born?

EDITH. On Yom Kippur.

RUTH. What?

PRIORESS. The—

EDITH. —The Hebrew Day of Atonement when—

PRIORESS. —And you believe that your being born on the Day of Atonement will set you in my eyes above the other applicants?

EDITH. No. But I wish to atone for those who will not atone. The heartless followers of Chancellor Hitler. I know I am nothing, but God cannot be satisfied with halfway measures. I offer my whole being so that the reign of the anti-Christ will end. And so that justice will be restored and fascism destroyed!

PRIORESS. Why have you become a Christian?

EDITH. That is a secret between me and God.

(Beat.)

PRIORESS. Have you ever committed a crime?

EDITH. I was born a Jew. Today that is a crime.

RUTH. You have a good deal of money at least.

EDITH. I have no money.

RUTH. (*Disbelieving.*) Reverend Mother!

EDITH. I am unemployed once more. I have no money.

PRIORESS. And yet you have not come to beg for food ...

RUTH. That's a bad sign, Reverend Mother. They are not humble. I remember how my father suffered after the war watching them flaunt their books and their jewels in the face of hunger and chaos!

(THE PRIORESS takes a wooden clapper hanging from her waist and shakes it—wood on wood, a sharp sound used to maintain discipline. Instantly, SISTER RUTH falls to her knees in front of The Prioress.)

PRIORESS. Sister Ruth! Our own mother, Teresa of Avila, descended from Spanish Jews.

RUTH. But Reverend Mother, Father Conrad said. "Know ye Christians that next to the devil thou hast no enemy more cruel, more venomous and violent than a true Jew!"

PRIORESS. We are straying from the prescribed questions.

EDITH. The Crown of Heaven herself was a Jew, as was her Son, whom I was born to wed.

PRIORESS. Do you feel you are the equal to men?

EDITH. Oh, in the temporal world, a woman can fill any position a man can, if she is healthy.

PRIORESS. Even the priesthood?

EDITH. Women were ordained deacons in the primitive church.

PRIORESS. Are you a feminist?

RUTH. A what?

PRUDENCE. A feminist is a woman who is feminine in the extreme.

EDITH. As a well-known convert put it. After faith has come, there is neither Jew nor Greek, neither bound nor free, there is neither male nor female. ...

PRIORESS. However, temptation first came to a woman.

EDITH. Yes. And God's first message of grace was also announced to a woman. And in both cases the YES pronounced by the woman decided the fate of all mankind. Our Lord had women among His most intimate friends.

PRIORESS. What led to your conversion, Edith?

EDITH. By chance I found the life of St. Teresa of Avila in a friend's library. The more I read that night, the more I began to feel myself filled with light. I no longer felt barren. At dawn, when I finally put it down, I said to myself, "This is the truth." It confirmed my own experience—it's not acquiring great knowledge that counts—God does not reveal His mysteries to the mind, but to the heart that surrenders itself to Him, without prejudices, fear, pride. Since then I've known there is something for me here I can't find anywhere else. I no longer fear death.

PRIORESS. Then you are not here to seek sanctuary from the woes befalling your people?

EDITH. No.

PRIORESS. Because if that were the case, we could find a room for you.

EDITH. No. I am not here to flee from the world. But to bear the Cross for those who are in the world. I do not expect to be left in peace here for long. Time is short. Please, pull back the curtain now. It reminds me too much of those frightening days after the war when I couldn't get work anywhere.

RUTH. My father couldn't find work after the war either. And there were fifteen of us.

EDITH. It must have been difficult for you to continue your studies, Sister Ruth.

RUTH. Yes.

EDITH. If German women were better educated we wouldn't be in the midst of such disquiet.

RUTH. My baby sisters have joined the League of German Girls.

EDITH. They must have formal schooling. I will find a way for them to become educated. My mother will help, I know.

RUTH. (*Surprised, touched.*) Thank you.

PRIORESS. I know you have no money, but do you at least possess a dozen handkerchiefs?

(THE NUNS laugh at this inside joke.)

PRIORESS. Sister Ruth cried every day her first two weeks here.

RUTH. The handkerchiefs are still here and you may use them, if you are admitted.

PRUDENCE. Do you enjoy parties?

EDITH. I love parties.

PRIORESS. Do you cook?

EDITH. No.

RUTH. Do you sew?

EDITH. No.

PRUDENCE. Do you sing?

EDITH. No.

PRUDENCE. Do you have a temper?

EDITH. Yes!

PRIORESS. Are you ready to be corrected publicly for your faults?

EDITH. With God's grace.

PRIORESS. Would you see the will of God in the decisions of your superiors?

EDITH. I should try—with all my heart.

PRIORESS. There is one final requirement. A test which all applicants must pass. You should offer a song as a gift to the heart of Jesus. In celebration.

EDITH. A song?

RUTH. Anything you want to sing.

EDITH. I'm sorry. I can't sing.

PRIORESS. Just a bar or two. It's the intention that counts, not the vocal ability.

EDITH. But I can't ... I have never been able to ...

PRUDENCE. You must. It matters a great deal to us.

EDITH. But my being admitted can't depend ...

PRUDENCE. Sing dear.

EDITH. I'm sorry. It's impossible. I know the catechism by heart. Ask me anything ... (*SHE begins to sing with great difficulty.*)

"O ... Come, O, Come, Emmanuel
And ransom captive Israel
Who lies in mournful exile here
Until the Son of God appear."

(*THE NUNS join her, singing in full voice.*)

"Rejoice! Rejoice! Emmanuel Shall come to thee O
    Israel—"

(*Crossfade to:*)

Scene 6

The Ministry of Church Affairs. KARL-HEINZ enters wearing a priest's cassock. FRANZY enters and kneels at his feet.

FRANZY. Bless me, Father, for I have sinned. It has been ten years since my last confession.

KARL-HEINZ. What are your sins?

FRANZY. Isn't it enough that I haven't been to confession for ten years? Don't you think I merit a stiff penance? Give me a severe penance, Father.

(KARL-HEINZ pushes him away. FRANZY bursts into laughter. KARL-HEINZ begins to strip off his cassock.)

FRANZY. What a brilliant idea, Karl-Heinz! To violate the sanctity of the confessional! Everyone in the Ministry is buzzing with this. You have a great vocation for Church Affairs. Before long you will rise in the Party to the role of Bishop. Then Archbishop. And, if you keep up the good work, who knows? You may become a Prince of the Church!

KARL-HEINZ. I like it.

FRANZY. What next?

KARL-HEINZ. Convents.

(Crossfade to:)

Scene 7

Edith's home. SHE is preparing to leave for the convent and is packing her suitcase and wooden boxes. SHE

*packs only one thing—books. There are books all over
the parlor floor. EDITH sits on the floor surrounded by
them, packing each one with great care and tenderness.
It is very late at night. FRAU STEIN enters, using an
elegant walking stick. Although older now, FRAU
STEIN never looked more like an empress, impeccably
dressed and combed, her back ramrod straight, we see a
woman of great discipline. For this meeting with her
beloved daughter, FRAU STEIN has summoned up her
considerable physical and spiritual strength. EDITH
does not see her mother enter. FRAU STEIN watches
EDITH use a dust cloth on a book.*

FRAU STEIN. It is a terrible world
EDITH. Oh, Mother. Thank you for coming down.
FRAU STEIN. I am not a savage. What do you want of
me, Edith?
EDITH. Your blessing. (*Pause.*) I've set aside some of
my old things in this basket. You might want some of
them—for when you visit your poor people. (*SHE pulls
out her Medal of Valor—gold with a red cross in its center
hung on a red sash.*) One of the children might enjoy this.
FRAU STEIN. Your Medal of Valor?! I'll keep that
myself, thank you.
EDITH. I need your blessing, Mother.
FRAU STEIN. In fact, I'll put it on right now. I
suffered right along with you during the war. Show me the
rest. (*SHE pokes scornfully through Edith's old clothes
with her walking stick.*) My goodness! I used to make you
such pretty clothes—this skirt looks just like a horse
blanket! You haven't packed any of your clothes....?
EDITH. No, Mother.
FRAU STEIN. You will change your mind.
EDITH. Oh, Mother. You won't forget to send the
scholarship money to Sister Ruth's family?

FRAU STEIN. I have already sent the first installment.

EDITH. How generous you are.

FRAU STEIN. Those women are taking you from me.

EDITH. It is my choice.

FRAU STEIN. No one will drive you to the train.

EDITH. Say that you love me, Mother. Say that you bless me.

FRAU STEIN. You ask for too much.

EDITH. Too much? Don't you know leaving you is the greatest sacrifice anyone has ever asked me to make?

FRAU STEIN. Then why do it?

EDITH. I must.

FRAU STEIN. Is it such a great sacrifice to leave me? Maybe you're telling yourself it is, but I've never seen such a look in your eyes! Like a bride on her wedding day. If it's sacrifice you want, stay. (*Beat.*) No. Don't stay. This is not a house for martyrs. Has my life meant nothing to you? What did I do the day your father died? Install a telephone. I was the first woman to have a business telephone in Breslau! Why? Because I had so many children to feed. I didn't sit and suffer. I made your father's lumberyard flourish. I trained myself to look at whole forests and know in a second what they're worth. (*Beat.*) But you have not thought of these things because you are not thinking. There is nothing of your head in this—for the first time in your life. There is something shameless in this passion of yours. I should chain you to that chair until this fever passes.

EDITH. How well you know me, Mother. Give me a strait jacket before I fly apart. Or some heavy thing that will press me down and contain me—

FRAU STEIN. —If you want a cross, get married. Life will hold you down.

EDITH. No matter how important I was regarded in the world, one telephone call from you and my legs would turn to water, I could hardly speak. Why is that? Nothing, nothing, nothing affects me more than you. Just being in the same room, I begin shaking all over at my age ... why is that? Any thoughts of plans, hopes—

FRAU STEIN. Tea, Edith. Tea is a blessing at such moments. Serve the tea.

(EDITH goes to a large samovar and serves her mother a cup.)

FRAU STEIN. That time in school, when you were still such a little child. We didn't speak about it then. The time you thought you were going to get the Schiller Prize. You'd told me you were the first in your class that year. You promised you would make me a present of your Schiller Prize.

EDITH. I *was* first in my class.

FRAU STEIN. But the professor gave the prize to Matilde Schlager.

EDITH. I'm glad he did. Matilde had no father.

FRAU STEIN. *I* was a widow.

EDITH. You were a father *and* a mother.

FRAU STEIN. The professor ... he was anti-Semitic.

EDITH. Yes, Mother, he was.

FRAU STEIN. Edith, you are anti-Semitic.

EDITH. (*Pause.*) I am still a Jew, Mother. It's true that my knowledge of Judaism is shamefully limited. But I plan to learn. I will learn. I am much less prejudiced now than I once was about spiritual matters. You always worried so much about me because I had no faith. I grow in faith. And, I hope, in love. I can't tell you how much more I love what we are, appreciate so our family, our ways. One of the many myths about Paul the Apostle—

FRAU STEIN. —His name was Saul. His name was Saul. Do not change his name!

EDITH. It is claimed that he repudiated his Jewish Heritage to become a Christian. This is not so. In his mind, he—

FRAU STEIN. —Why haven't we spoken of these things before? Because we cannot speak of them.

EDITH. Then I cannot remain here. I don't want to hurt you, Mother!

FRAU STEIN. Then I am less important to you than these things you have learned in the world.

EDITH. I must give up everything and follow Him.

FRAU STEIN. How cruel He is.

EDITH. You can rent my room.

FRAU STEIN. If there is one thing I'm going to teach you before you leave this house, that is a small measure of tact. You haven't a drop of it. You may have learned many things in your fine books, my dear, but a book on tact you've never read. No. You cannot leave here until you have learned tact....!

EDITH. Yes, Mother.

FRAU STEIN. Who would rent your room? What am I to tell people?

EDITH. How many times have I had to leave you already? The university, the war, teaching, lecture tours, retreats ...

FRAU STEIN. But you have always come back!

EDITH. Carmelite nuns, Mother, are often thought of as one person in the role of Moses, raising his arms to heaven, interceding for the people on the plain, and singing the glory of God in the name of mankind.

FRAU STEIN. Carmelites! How dare they assume they have the power for prayer that men have. Carmel—Oh, how they steal everything from us. Carmel, Edith, is a small mountain in Palestine. The Prophet Elijah went there to seek God in solitude and to pray for his people— nine-hundred years before He was born!

EDITH. Elijah founded the Carmelite Order!

FRAU STEIN. Tact! Edith. Tact! Or I shall wash out your mouth with soap!

EDITH. Oh, you are your old self again! Here, strike my fingers the way you used to. Go on. I know you want to. Strike them hard. It would please me to become a child again.

(FRAU STEIN kisses Edith's palm. Then, throws her arms around her child and begins to sing Edith a Yiddish lullaby.)

FRAU STEIN. Oh, my Edith. Always so eager to please me and never knowing how. You are a spinster. Alone. And as my youngest daughter your place is here with me. It is unnatural for an unmarried woman to be leaving her home, taking only boxes of worn out, old books.

EDITH. They are my dowry.

FRAU STEIN. Dowry? I don't understand.

EDITH. Come to my wedding, and you shall understand.

FRAU STEIN. Wedding?

EDITH. Parents and friends are permitted to attend the ceremony when a young woman takes the veil.

FRAU STEIN. You are not young.

EDITH. I shall cease to be a spinster and become a bride of Christ. And, before the world, I shall wear His gold wedding ring.

FRAU STEIN. *(Pushes aside the books with her walking stick.)* Books, books, books. How I pity you. Those pathetic old books are no dowry.

EDITH. They are my greatest treasure.

FRAU STEIN. I will give you a rich dowry.

EDITH. You have. You have. You have given me so much.

FRAU STEIN. I will sew you a regal wedding dress.

EDITH. The nuns are sewing a beautiful dress for me. You are so generous.

FRAU STEIN. Apparently I have given you nothing.

EDITH. I have never felt more Jewish than now.

FRAU STEIN. Then stay!

EDITH. And join an order of Jewish nuns? Where are they? With the other Jewish women left behind in the women's section of the Synagogue, watching behind cheese cloth drapes as the men go toward the altar. That's not close enough for me. There is nothing for me to do on the altar of the Synagogue.

(FRAU STEIN slaps her face. SHE turns from Edith.)

FRAU STEIN. After the war you should never have told me you had become a Christian. I have been mourning a dead child for so many years. I hoped that by some miracle I might have raised the dead. You are mad. Nothing good can come to you. What are you going to do with the Carmelite sisters?

EDITH. Live with them.

FRAU STEIN. And never was there anyone so left-handed in the kitchen! What will they think of you?

EDITH. It will be a trial period.

FRAU STEIN. You will go through with it to the very end. I know. You are even more obstinate than I am.

EDITH. For the disease of stubbornness there is no cure. Give me your blessing, Mother.

FRAU STEIN. I will never see you again. *(Pause.)* The family history that you have been putting together ... I don't see it anywhere. Where is it? Perhaps I can finish it.

EDITH. I will finish it. I was working on it. I have it right here. (*SHE presses the manuscript to her breast.*) I'll carry it myself. I don't want to lose it.

FRAU STEIN. (*Starts to leave.*) Edith, the Rabbi's sermon today, it was beautiful, wasn't it?

EDITH. Yes.

FRAU STEIN. Then it is possible for a Jew to be pious?

EDITH. Certainly.

FRAU STEIN. A convert is no Jew and no gentile. I don't want to say anything against Him. He may have been a very good man. But why did He make Himself a God?! (*SHE exits.*)

(*Crossfade to:*)

Scene 8

Chanting. THE NUNS enter carrying tall, lighted candles and circle around EDITH. THEY stand the candles on the floor and help EDITH to undress to her slip. Then THE NUNS help EDITH to put on a beautiful wedding gown. THE NUNS pick up the candles and EDITH passes through them, stopping in front of THE PRIORESS, who presses a simple, wooden cross to Edith's lips.

PRIORESS. This plain wooden cross has no corpus on it because in spirit you will take Our Lord's place there. On earth you will perpetuate the suffering life of Our Lord. With Christ you are nailed to the cross.

RUTH. There is nothing in the valley or house or street worth turning back for. Nothing.

EDITH. Passion of Christ, comfort me. (*SHE takes the cross and with great yearning kisses it a long while.*)

PRIORESS. What do you ask for?

EDITH. The mercy of God, the poverty of the Order, and the company of the Sisters.

PRIORESS. Are you resolved to persevere in the Order until death?

EDITH. Thus do I hope and desire, through the mercy of God and the prayers of the Sisters.

(We hear the martial strains of "Deutschland Uber Alles," the German national anthem. Suddenly, KARL-HEINZ, FRANZY, and OTHER SOLDIERS in dress uniform appear among THE NUNS, enacting their own ceremony. The MUSIC swells to the end of the scene, engulfing the convent ceremony.)

FRANZY. Harsh and pitiless are the laws of the Order. In spirit we are isolated from pseudo-men. Above good and evil. The universe is only an illusion that can be altered, perfected by the strength of your will.

PRIORESS. Receive the sweet yoke of Christ and His burden, which is light. In the name of the Father, and of the Son, and of the Holy Ghost.

KARL-HEINZ. I swear by God this sacred oath, that I will render unconditional obedience to Adolf Hitler, the Fuhrer of the German Reich and people, Supreme Commander of the Armed Forces, and will be ready as a brave soldier to risk my life at any time for this oath.

EDITH. Please help me to be worthy of living at the heart of the Church's holiness ... and to offer myself for those who are in the world. Please help me. I wish to take the name Teresa Benedicta of the Cross.

(FRANZY slowly begins to raise a sword over Karl-Heinz.)

FRANZY. All your energies are directed toward changing life on earth.

PRIORESS. In order to arrive at knowing everything, desire to know nothing.

KARL-HEINZ. I am embarking on an irreversible, superhuman destiny.

EDITH. In order to arrive at possessing everything, desire to possess nothing.

(As the scene builds to its climax, EDITH and KARL-HEINZ speak simultaneously.)

EDITH.	KARL-HEINZ.
In order to arrive at everything, desire to be nothing.	
Desire to be nothing.	Superhuman destiny.
Desire to be nothing.	
Desire to be nothing.	Destiny ...
Desire, Desire,	Destiny,
Desire,	Destiny ...
Desire ...	

The Curtain Falls

ACT II

Scene 1

THE PRIORESS and DR. SAUL WEISMANN enter.

WEISMANN. Did Dr. Stein ever return to the place of her birth?

PRIORESS. Yes, she did. The transport train that brought her to Auschwitz was delayed in the Breslau rail yard a few hours that night. While the engine was being refueled a guard slid open one of the doors of the cattlecar. A nun wearing a Star of David appeared at the opening and told him, "Those are the lights of my hometown. I will never see it again."

WEISMANN. Others suffered. Why single her out?

PRIORESS. I don't know. Something about her lingers in the mind.

WEISMANN. You know you do not belong here, Reverend Mother.

PRIORESS. We have planted flowers and fruit trees in our garden. Please, I want you to see them.

(THEY go to the imaginary garden.)

PRIORESS. Oh, look at those beautiful butterflies! Have you seen that room across the way, where a group of small children were held? The one with the butterflies scratched all over the walls? I can't forget it.

WEISMANN. Neither can I.

PRIORESS. How did they know they were going to die? But they knew it because they scrawled good-byes to

49

their mothers and fathers, and, then, filled the room with those exuberant, farewell butterflies. (*SHE looks at darting butterflies.*) Is it possible that small butterflies darting and dancing about are the souls of very small children? Oh, I know it's blasphemy to think that, but I'm always looking for continuity.

WEISMANN. How long do butterflies live? How long do flowers exist? If you've been in the camps, you don't grow old. The heart gives out. Were human bodies made to bear such fear? The cost of this catastrophe to us is incalculable. Last week I lost a friend. He was like a brother to me. He died of a heart attack. Although we were here together, he never could bring himself to talk about it. Your flowers are having a bad effect on me, I'm sorry. I don't know why I said what I just did about all of us not growing old. I plan to grow very old. I have a lot to do.

PRIORESS. You were here? At Auschwitz?

WEISMANN. As a child.

PRIORESS. I thought all the children were killed?

WEISMANN. I convinced them I was a man. I showed them I was a man.

PRIORESS. How?

WEISMANN. The boy ahead of me being examined by the camp doctor our first day pretended to have all sorts of ailments, imagining the physician would take pity on him. Instead, I saw him dragged out and kicked to death. When my turn came, the doctor fastened his eyes on me. I had a painful boil under my arm. He sunk a scalpel into it. I didn't cry out or show the slightest discomfort during the rest of that examination. I passed the first test. (*Beat.*) Every week we were stripped, examined. Every week men were marked for execution. I worked hard on a road gang. As a reward, I became one of the gardeners at the crematorium. The flowers were particularly beautiful there.

PRIORESS. God wanted you to live.

WEISMANN. But not my family. I was working in front of the crematorium planting seedlings in the sunlight when I saw them: my mother, my father, my sister. They were marching to their deaths.

PRIORESS. Did they see you?

WEISMANN. Our eyes met ... for an eternity.

PRIORESS. You have a strong heart, sir.

WEISMANN. I know why I am alive: to see to it that you understand that fully one-third of the world's Jews were slaughtered. We are small in number and we cannot lose one, or the memory of one. Madame, we Jews don't descend from a god or some aristocrat, but from a band of runaway slaves. The Exodus was just as important as Auschwitz! The destruction of Jerusalem by Romans was just as important as Auschwitz! This tragedy—hammered into the body of our people—is of cosmic import to us—and I stake claim, yes, claim to our tragic rights to the unmitigated misery experienced here. (*Beat*) Yes, yes, non-Jews suffered here, but a convent in this place clouds over the magnitude of our catastrophe. And to name this convent for a convert only compounds the problem. How can her name be coupled with ours here at Auschwitz?

PRIORESS. Sister Teresa was always difficult, I admit. Quite difficult.

(*Crossfade to:*)

Scene 2

NUNS begin chanting.

"Behold how good and pleasant it is to dwell together in harmony. It is as the dew that comes down from the mountains of Zion."

THE PRIORESS moves from Weismann to THE NUNS, who lie on the floor, head down, arms spread out like a cross. This penitential ritual is known as THE CHAPTER OF FAULTS. When each NUN confesses SHE remains on her stomach, but rises her head and torso, chanting her fault—or the fault of another nun— on one note.

RUTH. In Charity, I accuse Sister Prudence of taking her hands out of her sleeves, walking with them swinging at her sides, and of breaking the Great Silence.

PRUDENCE. In Charity, I accuse Sister Ruth of breaking silence during din ... ner. She asked me to pass her the wa ... ter. I would have passed it to her in any case, if she'd had the patience to wa-ai-t.

EDITH. (*Tries to chant.*) In Charity, I accuse myself of failure in my needlework. (*Takes a big breath.*) Of wasting thread ... of not progressing beyond the beginner's stage (*Speaks.*) Oh, I have ruined the Christmas vestments entrusted to me!

(The formal CHAPTER OF FAULTS deteriorates.)

RUTH. This may be the last Christmas we will ever be able to enjoy. The Fuhrer is saying Christmas should be replaced by a pagan Yulfest! And people are taking down the crucifixes in schools and office buildings putting the Fuhrer's picture there instead!

EDITH. Where is the peace on earth? Peace on earth to men of good will. But not all are of good will. And to them the Prince of Peace does not bring peace but the sword.

PRUDENCE. And not a moment too soon! An agent of the devil has stolen the Christ child from the Christmas manger in the Cathedral! Reverend Mother, that Infant is five-hundred years old. How can men be so wicked?

EDITH. You must have a very special gift for Our Lord this Christmas, Sister Prudence.

PRUDENCE. Not very special, not very new. What I give Him every morning, every night. Just Sister Prudence. But totally. What else can I give Him but myself?

EDITH. May I help you with the cooking?

(THE PRIORESS exchanges a wide-eyed look with the NUNS.)

PRIORESS. Uhhhhh thank you, Sister, but I have burdened you with domestic duties long enough. I want you to go back to your intellectual work. Translations, perhaps. Or a life of St. Elizabeth of Hungary. And then you can have your work published. Germany is in need of such literature.

EDITH. Reverend Mother, allow me to continue with my domestic duties. They are a penance for me. But may I also have time to continue work on my family history?

PRIORESS. You have my permission.

(EDITH takes out a letter.)

EDITH. I have a letter for my mother. Would you read it and send it? And please, don't use any Hitler stamps.

PRIORESS. She has not answered one of your letters all these years. Why have you persisted in writing her?

EDITH. Because I love her.

PRIORESS. I will read it and send it.

EDITH. Pardon me, Reverend Mother. Has the mail came today?

PRIORESS. Yes.

EDITH. And there was nothing for me?

PRIORESS. No.

EDITH. But do you know why the Holy Father has not acknowledged my letter to him?

RUTH. You wrote to the Pope yourself!?

PRIORESS. With my permission, Sister Teresa wrote to His Holiness, imploring him to write an encyclical on the suffering of her people.

EDITH. I met him when I was teaching. I know him. He will believe me. (*SHE takes the small stool and sits behind the grille, opening a small prayer book on her lap.*)

Scene 3

KARL-HEINZ enters the convent parlor. HE likes the silence, the mystery of the place. EDITH senses someone is in the parlor, puts her prayer book down.

EDITH. Come close to the grille. Are you hungry? Don't be afraid. May we help you? (*Pause.*) Praised be Jesus Christ.

KARL-HEINZ. Praised be Jesus Christ.

EDITH. Now and forever.

KARL-HEINZ. That's sort of like, "Good morning, how are you?"

EDITH. Very well, thank you.

KARL-HEINZ. Everybody used to say that when I was a boy. A kind of greeting.

EDITH. And they don't say that anymore?

KARL-HEINZ. What?

EDITH. "Good morning, how are you?"

KARL-HEINZ. No. Praised be Jesus Christ

EDITH. Now and forever.

KARL-HEINZ. I'm beginning to enjoy this.

EDITH. It's been so long since I've been in the world, I thought, perhaps ...

KARL-HEINZ. It's quiet here. It smells nice

EDITH. You smell of liquor.

KARL-HEINZ. Ah, the only scent worthy of a man.

EDITH. I had forgotten how overpowering the smell of spirits can be.

KARL-HEINZ. Do you pray for the intentions of soldiers here?

EDITH. We pray for the intentions of everyone. We desire to envelop all mankind in one single embrace ... including the abandoned, the repulsive, the criminal.

KARL-HEINZ. That doesn't work, loving too many people at one time.

EDITH. But we do have a special place in our hearts here for our heroes, our veterans.

KARL-HEINZ. Then you are patriotic here?

EDITH. We try to remember our disabled heroes in our prayers. The physically and spiritually deformed need the faith and courage of special prayers.

KARL-HEINZ. Pain opens our hearts.

EDITH. We take these men in our arms. They are in despair.

KARL-HEINZ. Would you pray for my intentions?

EDITH. If your intentions are not incompatible with Christian charity.

KARL-HEINZ. What makes you think they're not?

EDITH. Are you a soldier? You must pray for me. I'm about to take my final vows. I will need them.

KARL-HEINZ. Praying is your profession, not mine.

EDITH. What is your profession?

KARL-HEINZ. No one ever asked me to pray for them.

EDITH. What are your intentions?

KARL-HEINZ. I represent the Ministry of Church Affairs.

EDITH. Why are you here?
KARL-HEINZ. Describe yourself.
EDITH. What kind of work do you do?
KARL-HEINZ. The same as you. God's work. By cleansing the nation of the Jewish evil, I'm fighting for the Lord's work.
EDITH. Who are you?
KARL-HEINZ. Pray for me.
EDITH. Who are you?

(KARL-HEINZ goes. The LIGHTS change.)

Scene 4

HANNAH REINACH, holding an enormous bouquet of yellow flowers, is talking to EDITH through the grille. This is not the confident HANNAH we saw in Act I. SHE looks unkempt, wears a shabby coat, her hair is in disorder. In her anxious state, HANNAH unconsciously pulls apart the bouquet during the course of the scene.

HANNAH. The naked little boy couldn't have been more than five or six. There were a few families lunching at Maria Spring. Lots of children were running about, splashing in the water. But this little one caught my eye right away. Oh, he was having such a good time. He seemed like a clean, white bird, waving his wings in and out of the water when two men, fully dressed, waded into the water and—*(Beat)* Edith, he was a brave, strong boy. It was a beautiful day. How his body and his wet hair shone in the sun! For a moment I thought it was some sort of game. Was he laughing? Was he crying? Was he laughing? The men plunged his head under the water and held it there by force. I think I went insane suddenly. "He was circumsized," one of them said.

EDITH. I'm glad you came today, Hannah.

HANNAH. Are you? I couldn't come before. I haven't had the strength. I wish you could pull back the curtain, Edith.

EDITH. Did you bring me a copy of Professor Reinach's book?

HANNAH. Oh, dear. It doesn't matter that he died a Christian soldier ... fighting for his country. It is of no importance to anyone that he was a brilliant man. No. Today it is enough that he was a biological Jew. That is the only thing that matters. (*Beat.*) You worked so hard on his papers, Edith. I'm sorry. I have tried,—but no one will publish them.... No. So I have stopped trying....

EDITH. How is my mother?

HANNAH. ... I have stopped trying

EDITH. Let me get you some water, Hannah. We have a deep well with cool, fresh water.

HANNAH. No! Don't go. Please.

EDITH. Are you all right? I'll be right back.

HANNAH. Can you come out here?

EDITH. No.

HANNAH. I've become like an old woman these last few years, Edith. Why, I don't even comb my hair anymore. And yet, the older I become, the more I feel like a small, frightened child. There is no one to gather me up in their arms and make me feel safe anymore. Can't you come out, even a minute? I want someone to smooth down my hair

EDITH. How is my mother?

HANNAH. You sound so calm, dear. I'm speaking too loudly, I know. I'll try to whisper. I've been training myself to speak softly. But, even so, no matter where I go, I feel heads turning my way, stares ... it's almost impossible to change the voice you were born with. (*Beat.*) You are so safe here, Edith.

EDITH. I do not think I will be left in peace for long.

HANNAH. All this silence! I almost forgot, I brought flowers. Do you pray ... for my husband's soul, Edith?

EDITH. Hannah, I ... First, put the flowers on the turntable next to the grille. We'll put them on the altar right away.

HANNAH. Turntable? Oh, dear. I had not come before because I was afraid this would be like a medieval dungeon, and to me, it is ... this is like a fortress where Christian knights tortured poor Jewish souls five-hundred years ago.

EDITH. Hannah ...

HANNAH. Forgive me, Edith. I don't know what's been happening to me lately. Heaven seems so far away from me these days. Sometimes I look for Reinach and do not find him. And, then, somehow, I know he is here. That with your powerful mind you command him to yourself! That you have taken him from me somehow...!

EDITH. Hannah, have you been able to see my mother?

HANNAH. I don't know if you are the most selfish person I've ever known, or the most selfless...!

EDITH. I want to forget myself—

HANNAH. —Forget yourself! What else do you have to do here but think of yourself!

EDITH. I don't know if I'll ever be worthy of living in this place.

HANNAH. You frighten me.

EDITH. But, Hannah, it all started with you. You had something I wanted. (*Pause.*)

HANNAH. I feel like the cow that has just given some milk and then kicks over the pail.

EDITH. I have not taken my final vows yet, Hannah.

HANNAH. I do not think I will come here again. I thought I'd find something of Reinach here. I was mistaken.

EDITH. My mother!?

HANNAH. She is not well. How can she be well? She is an outcast. Go to her. Help her.

EDITH. I am here for her sake. I have never felt closer to her than now. Oh, Hannah, I remember the wonderful gatherings we used to have in my house when I was growing up. Every night thirty people at least sat around Mama's big dining room table. People of all religions. Oh, Hannah, I would give my life if Jews and gentiles could sit together at a table like Mama's and break bread together.

HANNAH. It will never happen.

EDITH. I pray it will.

HANNAH. It would be a miracle. (*Beat.*) I have lost my faith in such things. I must go...

EDITH. Hannah !

HANNAH. Not Hannah. Anna. Anna, Sister Teresa. It's the Christian form of the name. The Eternal be with you— (*SHE goes.*)

EDITH. Hannah! Hannah !

(*HANNAH meets KARL-HEINZ as HE is about to enter the convent parlor. HE removes his hat.*)

KARL-HEINZ. Heil Hitler.
HANNAH. Praised be Jesus Christ.

(*KARL-HEINZ blocks her way.*)

KARL-HEINZ. Heil Hitler.
HANNAH. NOW AND FOREVER.

(SHE rushes by him and out. KARL-HEINZ enters the parlor.)

KARL-HEINZ. You believe in justice here? Fairness?

EDITH. Yes.

KARL-HEINZ. I thought so. I've come to engage you in fierce mental combat. If I win, you'll have to show me your face. *(Beat.)* Are you still there? Did I scare you off? It's only a word game.

EDITH. Will you promise to go and leave us in peace, if I win?

KARL-HEINZ. Agreed. But you won't. No woman has yet. There's a riddle I still remember from my school days. If you don't guess what I'm talking about, you'll have to pull back the curtain. Listen. I saw a woman flying. She had a beak of iron, a wooden body, and a feathered tail, bearing death. What did I see?

EDITH. A woman fleeing, with a beak of iron, a wooden body, and a butt of feathers bearing death ... is an arrow—once the companion of soldiers.

KARL-HEINZ. And what is a soldier?

EDITH. A slave. Didn't you know? Once a glorious slave. Now, he is just a slave chained by an oath to render unconditional obedience to a false messiah. A German soldier is less than a man.

KARL-HEINZ. What is a manless woman without a face?

EDITH. She is nothing.

KARL-HEINZ. And who are you?

EDITH. A slave.

KARL-HEINZ. In the service of a false messiah.

EDITH. In the service of love.

KARL-HEINZ. Please. Come out here. I want to see you.

EDITH. We have a strict vow of enclosure.

KARL-HEINZ. What do you look like? Where do you come from?

(THE PRIORESS enters behind Edith.)

PRIORESS. Sister Teresa!

KARL-HEINZ. Who's that?

EDITH. My superior.

KARL-HEINZ. Rank?

EDITH. General.

KARL-HEINZ. I want to get to know you better. I respect you nuns. Turning yourselves over to God makes sense. Nowadays, most men are so puny. But you probably haven't had the chance to meet—

PRIORESS.—Silence! I am the Prioress here.

KARL-HEINZ. Oh. The General.

PRIORESS. And this is spiritual headquarters, not a beer hall!

KARL-HEINZ. Name your weapons.

PRIORESS. Prayer, prayer, and more prayer.

KARL-HEINZ. Then your power terminates right here and now! I represent the Ministry of Church Affairs.

PRIORESS. I insist that you leave at—

KARL-HEINZ. Silence!

EDITH. Reverend Mother!

KARL-HEINZ. I wish to establish a visiting hour. We have received reports that our convents are hot beds of subversion.

PRIORESS. We strive for only one thing here.

KARL-HEINZ. What?

PRIORESS. Perfection.

KARL-HEINZ. Then let me in.

PRIORESS. This is madness!

KARL-HEINZ. Perfection? How can a woman tell if another woman is perfect? It takes a man to do that!

EDITH. Reverend Mother—

KARL-HEINZ. I want her out here.

PRIORESS. The aim of a woman when she enters a religious life is to surrender lovingly only to God!

KARL-HEINZ. I know. Don't you recognize my voice?

PRIORESS. That's blasphemy!

KARL-HEINZ. Listen. I've been thinking how nice it would be to convert this place into a dance hall for the League of German Girls. (*Beat.*)

PRIORESS. You may come for ten minutes every day at two.

KARL-HEINZ. Now, don't interrupt us.

(THE PRIORESS exits.)

KARL-HEINZ. Sister, are you there? I want to know you. (*Silence.*)

EDITH. I am the lowest form of human life, to you and your kind. Damnation by birth you'd call it.

KARL-HEINZ. I'll redeem you. I'll make you forget about original sin and all those pictures of hell they've put in your mind.

EDITH. You make me remember them.

KARL-HEINZ. You don't know how to talk to a man, do you? No, I guess you wouldn't get too much practice here. I didn't think women like you existed anymore. Every house should have a grille like this, with a heavy black curtain hanging over it. Then lovers could talk with one another as if they were lying side by side at night ... quietly, in the dark, free, invisible.

EDITH. Please go.

KARL-HEINZ. You Carmelites could teach us a thing or two about discipline, couldn't you? What a match that would be—the Elite Corps on one side and the Carmelites on the other, coming together to forge the highest form of human life. You are going to have to make room for us, you know, and not only in your prayers. These places make ideal offices, barracks, gymnasiums. You would be free then.

EDITH. Free?

KARL-HEINZ. What have you done? Why have you walled yourself up here?

EDITH. Why have you imprisoned yourself in the golden birdcage that is the city? Believe me when I say I see the light more clearly here.

KARL-HEINZ. Imprisoned myself?

EDITH. Damned! Damnation by choice I'd call it.

KARL-HEINZ. The choice is yours. Save me. Take me in your praying hands. The choice is yours. (*Pause.*) You can anoint my forehead for a start, with some cool, fresh water. And bathe my neck, my hands. My feet are burning. Yes, that would be nice. That's what I want you to do now. Give me a little baptism to cool me off. The air's as thick as a summer house. What are you hiding in there, a perfume factory?

EDITH. Just some flowers and fruit trees.

KARL-HEINZ. I'm waiting for you.

EDITH. I have not been in that parlor for five years. And I pray I never will be again.

KARL-HEINZ. The walls are perspiring, I swear.

EDITH. Last night I dreamed cinders were falling on my bed.

KARL-HEINZ. Bring me same water and a towel.

EDITH. We have a strict vow of enclosure.

KARL-HEINZ. I want you to wash my hands and feet. That's all.

EDITH. Why are you doing this?

KARL-HEINZ. I don't have to tell you what will happen to the women here if you don't came out.

EDITH. Yes, I know.

PRIORESS. (*Returns.*) Your time is finished for today. Go now. We will pray for you.

KARL-HEINZ. Praised be Jesus Christ.

PRIORESS. Now and forever.

(KARL-HEINZ leaves.)

PRIORESS. Take the man's visits as a sacrifice.

EDITH. Our sisters in Luxembourg were driven out of their convent by men such as he is! He is shameless. He will do anything to please himself. I am trying to warn you, Reverend Mother, because you are too innocent.

PRIORESS. Sister Teresa, remember your vows. We have bound ourselves to the enclosure, but God has not bound Himself to protect us in the enclosure walls forever. Certainly, we ought to pray that we shall be spared the experience, but only with the deeply sincere addition. "Not mine, but Thy will be done."

(Crossfade to:)

Scene 5

The Ministry of Church Affairs. It is Kristallnacht—the night when shop windows were broken at Jewish-owned businesses, and windows of sacred places of worship were shattered and the holy buildings were ransacked and burned. FRANZY is giving orders to a NAZI SOLDIER.

FRANZY. Spontaneous demonstrations are to be organized and executed this very night. Only such measures should be taken that do not involve danger to German life and property. Synagogues are to be burned down only when there is no danger of fire to the surroundings. Demonstrations should not be hindered by the police. There must be no cases of rape. The law forbids sexual intercourse between gentiles and Jews! Offenders will be expelled from the Party and turned over to the Civil Courts!

(NAZI SOLDIER salutes and exits. Crossfade to:)

Scene 6

EDITH encounters THE PRIORESS, who is holding an envelope.

EDITH. Oh, Reverend Mother, has the Holy Father sent me word?

PRIORESS. We must pray for your mother.

EDITH. If only she would pray for us. Her life is far more perfect than ours. I'm certain she is much closer to God then we.

PRIORESS. If what you say is true, then she is with God now, in His divine presence. She died late in the night.

(SHE hands EDITH a telegram. EDITH prays in Hebrew. [*] *)*

---

[*] The Mourner's Kaddish. "Yit-ga-dal ve-yit-ka-dash she-mei ra-ba be-al-ma di-ve-ra chi-re-u-tei, ve-yam-lich mal-chu-tei be-cha-yei-chon u-ve-yo-mei-chon u-ve-cha-yei de-chol beit/ Yis-ra-eil, ba-a-ga-la u-vi-ze-man ka-riv, ve-i-me-ru: a-mein."

EDITH. I would like my life to be like hers. What the Synagogue produced so can the Church. Can't it, Reverend Mother. Can't it?

PRIORESS. My child ... now there is nothing more for you in the world.

EDITH. I have never felt more in the world.

PRIORESS. I am your new mother.

EDITH. YOU ARE NOTHING LIKE MY MOTHER! (*Beat.*) Tact, Reverend Mother, I know.

PRIORESS. Not tact—silence. Silence of the mind, of the eyes, of the tongue. Your Hassidic people say, "Silence is a fence around wisdom."

EDITH. Speaking has always been a penance to me, Mother. Do I have your permission not to return to the grille? I need the time, for prayer, for thinking—to be by myself.

PRIORESS. There is always someone at the grille to comfort those who come for help. The grille is a test. It is a great responsibility. You have said yourself that women can perform priestly functions. Being at the grille is almost like being the priest in the confessional, who must learn to bear the burden of men's offenses against Christ.

EDITH. Reverend Mother, my presence here is a danger to the community!

PRIORESS. You will take your turn at the grille tomorrow.

(*Crossfade to:*)

Scene 7

EDITH moves to an imaginary confessional, kneels. KARL-HEINZ has taken the place of the priest on the other side of the imaginary partition, disguises his voice.

EDITH. Bless me, Father, for I have sinned. It has been one week since my last confession.

KARL-HEINZ. What are your sins?

EDITH. I have difficulty praying. I look for Our Lord on the cross ... I know He is there, but I do not see Him sometimes ... but now... there is a man, an officer ... whom, I know, needs me. Needs my prayers. He comes here day after day.

KARL-HEINZ. (*Pause.*) Yes?

EDITH. I cannot pray. I cannot pray for him.

KARL-HEINZ. You must pray for him ... You must love him.

Scene 8

The LIGHTS change. EDITH and KARL-HEINZ whirl about, are in the parlor and at the grille.

EDITH. You do not see me, you do not know me, why do you come here again and again and again?

KARL-HEINZ. I *have* seen you.

EDITH. How?

KARL-HEINZ. Certain informers—peasants, farmers— reported to me that on their way to market they always pass the convent at dawn and look up because there is a light at one of the windows, a flickering candle light. They told me they always see one of the nuns here standing at her window, with her arms outstretched like a cross, praying. I've come at different hours, late at night. And you are always there. Sister Teresa ... my Teresa ... my Teresan state of mind. Ah, Teresienstadt. When I go there,

I pretend it's been named after you. Teresa's City. Do you know what that is?

EDITH. Teresienstadt. Yes. A concentration camp. Not far. We've been praying for the people there.

KARL-HEINZ. To care about their welfare would be a crime against our own blood ... yours and mine.

(Crossfade to:)

Scene 9

EDITH moves to the privacy of her cell. Alone, SHE sits on the floor center stage, puts the manuscript of her family history on her lap. With great joy SHE starts reading it aloud.

EDITH. "We loved to play hide and seek on the piles of lumber behind Mama's office at the lumber yard. Elsa, because she was the eldest, refused to play. But Erna, Rosa, and I would coax our big brothers to chase us. Until one day I tore my dress...." (*SHE turns pages.*) "There was a particularly memorable birthday party for Mama that year. All of my father's twenty-five brothers and sisters and Mama's fifteen brothers and sisters arrived in Breslau from all over Germany. The house was filled with aunts and uncles and cousins. And neighbors, too. Especially those who shared a common garden with us: the Burgheims and their children...." (*SHE looks up.*) Fritz and Toni. (*Pause. EDITH closes the manuscript.*) Katya Krebs. The Lowenthals and their children. The Tropovitz family. The Liebermans. Rosa Guttman. Mrs. Blume. Irving and Lotte Rivitz. (*Pause.*) There isn't enough time. (*SHE rises her arms to heaven.*) There isn't enough time. Please, Lord heed my prayers.

Scene 10

EDITH remains immobile, with her arms outspread, as suddenly KARL-HEINZ, FRANZY, and THE NAZI SOLDIER, at the Ministry of Church Affairs begin to circle around her.

FRANZY. It's your duty to keep a stranglehold on the Church, not fondle just one of its members. Everyone here at the Ministry is starting to call you "Old Sacred Flame."

(FRANZY and THE NAZI SOLDIER laugh at KARL-HEINZ, who ignores them. The NAZI SOLDIER sinks his hands into a box HE has carried in containing religious objects.)

NAZI SOLDIER. Karl-Heinz, you should have been there this afternoon. We had a wonderful time going through all the hair shirts, habits, whips, and rosaries confiscated from that Carmelite convent in Luxembourg. *(HE tosses a rosary to FRANZY, who catches it.)*

FRANZY. What do you do at that convent every day at two in the afternoon?

NAZI SOLDIER. He's being far too secretive, Franz. Maybe it's a gypsy, or some lonely Jewess he's got hidden away.

FRANZY. If he brought her around, we'd make her welcome.

KARL-HEINZ. She is not a Jewess. She is not a gypsy.

FRANZY. Then, allow me to give you my congratulations. Ah, how fortunate to be in love at this time in our history. My blessings, Karl-Heinz, my

blessings to you both. Still, we have *other* convents to
look over.

(THE MEN leave swiftly.)

Scene 11

*THE NUNS pass through the MEN and circle EDITH,
carrying cleaning utensils: pails, soap, brushes, wash
cloths, brooms. The impression is of Edith in the
middle of a maelstrom. SISTER RUTH hands Edith a
pail and a brush. THE NUNS begin scrubbing the floor.
EDITH knocks over the pail, prostrates herself on the
floor in front of The Prioress.*

EDITH. Passion of Christ comfort me!

PRIORESS. Sister! You're trembling!

EDITH. His blood is the curtain by which we enter the
Holy of Holies.

PRIORESS. Sister, please, you must feel calm and free
in this marriage.

EDITH. This marriage can only be consummated on the
cross and sealed in blood for all eternity.

PRIORESS. Bloodshed is not the only sacrifice that
counts, but the service rendered is a daily martyrdom.

EDITH. God formed a covenant of blood with His
People on Mount Sinai I offer myself to the heart of Jesus
as a sacrificial expiation for the sake of true peace.

PRIORESS. What makes you think such a sacrifice
would ever be acceptable to Him?

EDITH. I know I am nothing, but God cannot be
satisfied with half-way measures.

PRIORESS. You do everything in extremes—by your
own rules. Sister, I know the zeal of converts is often

stronger than the zeal of those of us born to the faith. You must not feel that because you were born a Jew you must do these things. You must change your ways or leave this community.

RUTH. To eat sufficiently, to sleep contentedly, and to be thoroughly joyous, these are the true signs of a Carmelite's vocation.

PRUDENCE. Don't you think our convent is a little bit of paradise? Yes, I'm sure paradise must be like this.

EDITH. You are very good, Sister Prudence.

PRUDENCE. Oh, no Sister, I'm not. I'm too immodest. I ask for too much.

EDITH. What do you ask for, Sister Prudence?

PRUDENCE. Well, perhaps this will seem silly to you. But, when I die, if I go to heaven—I've been on my knees so long I would like Our Lord to give me a big red armchair to pray in.

EDITH. I'm sure Our Lord already has one picked out for you.

PRUDENCE. That would be nice.

EDITH. Reverend Mother, I beg, most humbly, your permission not to see the officer again.

PRUDENCE. This morning he sent us a basket of mirabelle plums.

PRIORESS. As I've told you, take the man's visits as a sacrifice.

PRUDENCE. Think of the good you are doing.

EDITH. Oh, Sister Prudence, you do not understand.

PRUDENCE Oh, I do. I do. You are the one who does not understand. Put yourself in his position. You wish to take up your dwelling in Christ and this officer wants to take up his dwelling in you. Now, surely, that shows he's on the right path.

EDITH. He is a wild beast.

PRUDENCE. All the better. Remember wild animals obeyed Saint Anthony. When the devil sent vicious hyenas to attack him, he simply dismissed them.

EDITH. Do I have permission to dismiss him, Reverend Mother? (*Beat. Tries to chant.*) In Charity, I accuse myself of—(*Speaks.*) He comes day after day, after day. I cannot pray. I cannot pray for him.

PRIORESS. Even the devil can be vanquished with love.

RUTH. Love is prayer.

EDITH. I cannot pray for him.

PRIORESS. Your prayers can do more for Germany than any soldier or politician.

EDITH. I cannot pray for him.

PRIORESS. It is clear to me now why your prayers for your people have come to nothing.

EDITH. What?

PRIORESS. We can deliver our bodies to be burned, but unless we do it for love there is no meaning to it.

EDITH. How...?

PRIORESS. How much simpler it is to love your people than to love this man who needs your prayers. You imagined that by offering your penances to God He would protect your people. But their suffering has only increased. Heaven has offered you the greatest test imaginable—to love your enemy—and you have failed. Unless you can take him in your praying hands, you will be unable to proceed to your final vows.

RUTH. We fight sin with all our strength, but love the sinner; intercede for those who murder Christ—even as they are murdering him.

PRIORESS. Yes, condemn the man's actions, but not the man. No one must be denied the hope of redemption. No one is without hope.

PRUDENCE. I offer my *life*—what little there is left of it—so that Sister Teresa will find the strength to redeem this man through love, surrender to God's will, and find some rest at last. (*SHE gets up and starts to leave. Turns.*) I am going to our garden to pick some white roses for Sister Teresa. I am going to make a crown for her to wear on the day she takes her final vows. (*SHE goes. Pause.*)

EDITH. I will love him. I will love him.

(*Crossfade to:*)

Scene 12

KARL-HEINZ, wearing a long, black cape, black gloves, rings the convent bell and enters the parlor. HE removes his hat. SISTER RUTH is at the grille.

RUTH. Is someone there? May we help you? Is someone there?

KARL-HEINZ. Yes. The postman.

RUTH. Oh. Sister Teresa is busy. I can't call her.

KARL-HEINZ. You have a voice like a telephone operator.

RUTH. I have my mother's voice.

KARL-HEINZ. I pity your father.

RUTH. He is a saint.

KARL-HEINZ. No doubt. No doubt. Look, I have work to do ...

RUTH. The devil's work. Amen. You see, I am not afraid of you. No, that's a lie. I am afraid of you. Amen.

KARL-HEINZ. Amen?

RUTH. Every word we say should be a prayer. I wish Sister Teresa would come!

KARL-HEINZ. Amen. Does she talk about me?
RUTH. Do you have large, dark, deep-set eyes?
KARL-HEINZ. Why do you want to know?
RUTH. And large, cavernous, flaring nostrils?
KARL-HEINZ. Why do you want to know?
RUTH. You smell like death, you must look like death.
KARL-HEINZ. Corrupt. Putrefying
RUTH. Please, stop.
KARL-HEINZ. I am splendid to behold. My great, black wings are spread over the entire convent, waiting to carry Sister Teresa away, far away to an open grave, where I will lay her down, gently ... where I can sleep with her for an eternity.

(Slight pause. SISTER RUTH begins weeping quietly.)

RUTH. I know. Poor Sister Teresa. We all have skulls in our cells to remind us that death is near, but they are nothing compared with you.
KARL-HEINZ. I don't know if you're being sincere or downright rude. Or if they are the same thing in this place. Now, call Sister Teresa, Sister ... uh?
RUTH. ... Ruth.
KARL-HEINZ. Go on. Call Sister Teresa. You hold no mystery for me, Sister Ruth.
RUTH. You hold no mystery for me, either.
KARL-HEINZ. Amen!
RUTH. Amen.
KARL-HEINZ. You're a brave girl. Now go.

(SISTER RUTH turns to leave. EDITH appears. SISTER RUTH falls into her arms, sobbing.)

EDITH. He's here?

(SISTER RUTH nods.)

RUTH. I'll stay with you.
EDITH. Go to the chapel and pray for us.

(SISTER RUTH leaves. EDITH goes to the grille.)

EDITH. Speak. I know you are there, invisible, shapeless. And yet you are closer to me than anything else. You have become an intimate part of us. You threaten our existence, take away our senses, paralyze us with fear.

KARL-HEINZ. But you like it. You consent to it.

EDITH. God has consented to it. He has permitted you to steal over my soul like a dark night, blotting Him out. I do not see Him on the cross. And I feel I am being annihilated when I am separated from Him. I know He is always there, but He is hidden from me and keeps silent. *(Touches the grille.)* I can only hear your voice now. Day and night. It is a test, a token of love awaiting love.

KARL-HEINZ. Love awaiting love?

EDITH. God's love.

KARL-HEINZ. You've been alone too long in this place.

EDITH. I was more alone throughout most of my years in the world, more alone than here, now.

KARL-HEINZ. With me. *(Pause.)* I have a letter from Rome ... *(HE takes it out.)*

EDITH. From Rome?

KARL-HEINZ. ... for "Sister Teresa Benedicta of the Cross." It came to the Ministry.

EDITH. I've been waiting a long time for that letter. And now it has come. Thank you for bringing it to me.

KARL-HEINZ. My pleasure.

EDITH. Pass it to me, please.

KARL-HEINZ. Oh, I can't do that. But, don't worry. I won't force you out here to get it. The day you come to me, it will be because you want to come to me.

EDITH. That day will never come.

KARL-HEINZ. I'm confident it will. It's a sweet sensation, a painful sensation, having to wait for a holy woman.

EDITH. Don't mock me.

KARL-HEINZ. Sister Teresa, you fill me with peace.

EDITH. The letter, please. It must be from the Holy Father.

KARL-HEINZ. It could be.

EDITH. Give it to me. (*Slight pause.*)

KARL-HEINZ. But you are my responsibility.

EDITH. Open it then.

KARL-HEINZ. All right. (*HE takes the letter out of the envelope.*) It's in Latin. His Holiness says he is most grateful that you wrote to him .... requesting that he write an encyclical on the problem ... of the Hebrews ... here. And his message to you is that he sends you and your family his blessings.

(*Pause.*)

EDITH. Is that all?

KARL-HEINZ. Yes. You needn't have written him. The problem is well in hand. (*Pause.*)

EDITH. There must be more in the letter. Something more.

KARL-HEINZ. No.

(*EDITH suddenly unfastens her collar, gasping for air. SHE is about to fall, but grabs hold of the grille.*)

KARL-HEINZ. You must do something about Sister Ruth. No respect for me at all! What have you told her about me? Saying that I am corrupt, that I am the angel of putrification and death—when everybody damn well knows it's you Carmelites who are the ones who sleep in coffins. (*Beat.*) Are you listening? Sister Teresienstadt? Sister Teresa?

EDITH. Sister Prudence! Sister Prudence ... I'm falling ... Sister Prudence I was standing in front of my cell window when ... I fall. (*Beat.*) Oh, my God, don't do this to me. (*Beat.*) Are you there? Listen to me. I don't want you here anymore. Just now, when you were reading that letter to me, you opened up a well of such hatred in me. Why have you done this to me? You have done what no one here has been able to do. How did you know it's not love I'm good for, but ... How wise, how wise the Holy Father must be to know that I'm not fit ... not fit to ask for anything. (*SHE begins to laugh, spreading her arms upward.*) How I pictured myself high up on top of a mountain interceding for the people suffering on the plain. How I wanted to raise my prayers to God. To perfect myself to be the perfect bride for Him, as any woman wants to perfect herself for the man she loves, so that he will do her bidding ... my bidding ... my ... unholy bidding. (*Beat.*) How did the Holy Father know ... I carry a hot stone of hate in me that pulls me down. It burns, God, how it burns. The desire to destroy you keeps my mind whirling day and night. (*Beat.*) I am being ... unchristian. I am being unchristian toward you. (*Beat.*) You see, there is no perfection in me. And the more imperfect I become, the more perfect you think I am. The more unnatural this dry, grotesque, perverted love of yours grows.

(*SHE sinks to the floor, sobbing. HE listens.*)

KARL-HEINZ. This hate of yours. I accept it, if that is all you can give me now. I'll relieve you of it gladly. I've built my strength carrying such burdens for many women. (*Beat.*) Of course, you don't consider yourself perfect. That's the first sign of perfection. If you consider me your ... enemy, that's simply because I am a man and you are becoming a woman again, a civilian. Good. (*Beat.*) I feel hope. I have never had bad thoughts. Do you know we used to think, when I was a boy, that if you had plenty of white dots on your fingernails it meant you were going to have many sons. I don't want to give you the wrong impression. One is all I want. Just one. Just one to be my eternity and enjoy the world I'll conquer for him. (*Beat.*) I do not want the child of an impure woman ... an imperfect woman. (*Beat.*) A woman carries a child only after he's conceived. For how long? Nine months. A man carries his son almost all his life. But his mother must be perfect. And where, but here, could I have found an ... exceptional woman? No, you're the woman for me. Strong, a proud bearing, and guaranteed. Otherwise, they would never have allowed you to live here. (*Beat.*) A kiss of peace is what I want. A kiss. No beggar will ever come to this convent as hungry as I am. Feed me. Don't you want to be ground by the teeth of a wild beast that you may be found pure bread?

EDITH. Yes.

KARL-HEINZ. Bend to me. Bathe my feet. Become humble in my sight.

(THE PRIORESS enters. SHE carries a bowl of water and a white cloth. SHE walks to Edith and bathes her forehead to refresh and comfort her.)

PRIORESS. Sister. Sister, are you prepared to take your final vows?

EDITH. When I have became an instrument not of hate but of peace then, perhaps ... (*EDITH covers her face with her veil and takes the bowl from The Prioress.*)

PRIORESS. Thank you for the example you have shown us from the first.

(*THE PRIORESS leaves. EDITH enters the parlor. LIGHT change. SHE walks in a half-circle, HE counters, as if the stage had turned. EDITH stops moving. Pause.*)

KARL-HEINZ. You know, I think I can feel your heart pounding all the way over here. (*Beat.*) I know you despise me, but I'm not really very ugly, am I? It's a pretty thing just to stand here and watch you breathe. The veil goes in, then the veil blows out.... Are you going to wash my feet?

(*Beat. HE gets a small stool, sits, sticks a foot out. EDITH walks to him, kneels in front of him. Puts the bowl of water down. As SHE bends her head over his boot, HE inserts a hand under her veil to touch her face The veil covers his hand. Suddenly, his hand shoots out from under her veil.*)

KARL-HEINZ. God! What's this? (*HE looks at his palm.*) Spit? Sweat? I thought you'd burned me. (*HE licks his palm.*) You're not ... I had tears in here, didn't I? (*Beat.*) I'm not going to harm you. I just want to see your face. (*HE uncovers her face.*) A difficult operation, giving a woman back her face again. If my hands are trembling it's because .... I've never been more alive than at this moment. You see, I'm drunk and shaking suddenly. (*HE moves away from her.*) You make me drunk and foolish and happy. Sister Teresa, why do you fear me? Trust me. I would change your life for another. I love you. (*Beat.*) I've seen a convent in Luxembourg. There's a small farm attached to it the nuns used for retreats. It's mine now. I've bought it. That's where I want to go with you....

EDITH. I do not want you. I never wanted you. Not you. Not a man who has imposed suffering ... on hundreds, on thousands ... on ... people not ... prepared to change their lives for another.

KARL-HEINZ. Jews only, for now. I do not handle the Aryan cases.

EDITH. Jews, only! Have you forgotten where you are? This is Christ's house.

KARL-HEINZ.The King of the Jews ...

EDITH. I AM A JEW. A Jew. (*SHE takes an identity card out of her pocket.*) There is no "J" on this identity card. No "Sara" before my name. All Jewish women are Saras. Write them in! In the Synagogue I learned exactitude at an early age. And through all my moments of belief and disbelief, the discipline of the Synagogue remained. Write them in!

KARL-HEINZ. If ... if we leave now, we can be in Luxembourg ... tomorrow ...

EDITH. WRITE THEM IN!

(With a primal yell, KARL-HEINZ raises a fist at her, but stops, turns from her.)

KARL-HEINZ. My father never trusted priests. But he sent me to a priests' school once, said they could teach me something. And they did. The first day. I was so nervous I couldn't stop talking. A priest was cleaning the blackboard, then suddenly stopped, walked toward me. He told me to stand up and ... open my mouth. He held the back of my head with one hand and stuffed the eraser cloth all the way into my throat and locked me in the closet where the coats were. (*HE begins to collapse on the small stool.*) I couldn't breathe, I couldn't cry ... It was dark in there and no air.

(*The LIGHTS begin to change. EDITH steps into her own light and slowly, through the following, begins to take off her nun's habit. As SHE removes each article of clothing SHE folds it lovingly, kisses it and places it on the floor at her feet until she is left wearing nothing but a shift which has a yellow Star of David sewn at her breast.*)

EDITH. Did you know that today is the feast of St. Peter in Chains? It has always been a special feast for me. Not because it commemorates anything in particular in my life, but because of the chains being loosed by angels' hands. How many chains have already been loosed, and what bliss it will be when the last ones fall.

Scene 13

EDITH is now in a bathhouse at Auschwitz, a chamber where the women undress before they take their showers. The women are a ghostly slow moving tableau of human suffering, like figures in a group sculpture by Rodin. The women are draped in gauzy, torn fabric, and it is hard to see their features. ALL, including EDITH are barefoot. Huddled in groups of two and three, EDITH tries to comfort them, sharing a meager ration of bread, raising a ladle of water to the lips of a frightened woman. THE PRIORESS and DR. WEISMANN enter and look at the scene, remaining to one side.

PRIORESS. Must our community no longer carry my child's sweet name?

WEISMANN. History has shown that we cannot compromise—ever again.

(KARL-HEINZ enters with HIS SOLDIERS.)

KARL-HEINZ. Collect all the wedding rings, crosses, rosaries and medals—any silver or gold they've got on them.

EDITH. Karl-Heinz. Karl-Heinz.

KARL-HEINZ. Stand three yards away. I thought Auschwitz would have defaced you. I hoped Auschwitz would have defaced you. But you are almost the only one in here who has a face. In five minutes you will be dead.

EDITH. Then in five minutes I will begin to live.

KARL-HEINZ. I've come to collect your valuables.

EDITH. My valuables?

KARL-HEINZ. Your gold wedding band.

EDITH. The new prisoners tell us you are making quite a profit selling the ashes of our people to their families back in Holland.

KARL-HEINZ. I'm an old Jew when it comes to business.

EDITH. You've learned nothing, have you?

KARL-HEINZ. I've forgotten nothing.

EDITH. Take the ring. It's a fair exchange. A tattoo for a ring.

(SHE hands him her wedding ring. HE takes her hand.)

KARL-HEINZ. Come out into the air. I cannot permit you to die with these others.

EDITH. Don't destroy my life!

(HE releases Edith's hand.)

EDITH. Thank you. The first weeks were frightening. Then, God's peace came to me. Now all is well.

KARL-HEINZ. I'll get you a priest.

EDITH. No, thank you. *(SHE begins to leave him.)* I rather like standing before my God this way ... Let Him see me in all my imperfections. Let Him see me as I am.

(THE WOMEN are now huddled in a group in the center of the stage. EDITH joins THE WOMEN, embraces them. TWO GUARDS appear above, put on gas masks. THEY toss pellets on the women, casting a golden glow over the chamber. THE WOMEN and EDITH freeze.)

PRIORESS. Our Church cannot compromise—but I can. I give you my word that in our remaining days here, this convent will no longer carry the name of Edith Stein.

WEISMANN. Thank you.

PRIORESS. If one gesture will help, well—perhaps, it will help her to rest. She never would have wanted to cause such fuss. Some food for your journey, Dr. Weismann. *(SHE hands him a package wrapped in brown paper.)* Or, as a favor to me, perhaps you would remain at table and we could break bread together.

(HE stares at her a short while, nods assent and BOTH exit. The golden light on THE WOMEN becomes a diminishing circle and transforms into a magical blue over the stationary WOMEN as we begin to hear FRAU STEIN's record of "The Beautiful Blue Danube.")

The Curtain Falls

PRODUCTION NOTES

The play works best on a unit set, flowing continually.
Simplicity is the key. Because the play is emotionally
large, it would be a mistake to think a large, costly
production is required. The human relationships are what
count. I have seen the play in tiny theaters, performed in
the round, and in large houses. A few candles held in the
hands of sincere actors can create magic. On stages that
have altitude, a bridge or upper level in the back of the
stage, has provided pictorial opportunities, but this is not
essential. *It is very important to engage the imagination of
the audience.* The imaginary convention is quickly
established when Dr. Weismann first enters and extends his
hand into the air and pulls down on an imaginary bell cord
and we hear the bell ring. Crucial is the imaginary grille.
Usually this is created by light—a diagonal shadow. But
the grille is basically created by the actors themselves.

COSTUMES. For many productions, the nearest
Carmelite convent has been very cooperative, in some
instances donating nuns' habits or actual fabric and other
information. It has proved to be very healthy to have the
actors visit a Carmelite convent during rehearsal. In every
instance, the actors were enriched, indeed, surprised by the
vitality and generosity of the nuns—which dispels notions
of any sort of depressing or joyless existence in a cloister.
Nazi uniforms and boots are usually rented.

MUSIC. There is always a choir master near at hand
who is happy to spend a day or two teaching the actors the
simple chants. To increase volume, the actors have been
recorded during singing rehearsal and this is played in the
background while the actors augment this by singing on
stage. FRAU STEIN's recording of "The Beautiful Blue

Danube Waltz" is best performed by the Berlin Philharmonic. The nice thing about it is that it has a long introduction, beautiful and not often heard. Particularly in the final, Auschwitz scene, it is wise to work with the introduction—and leave the familiar portion for the curtain call. The waltz during the curtain call is important because it provides an emotional release for the audience. Don't be surprised if for a second or two there is no applause. The audience usually sits stunned, holding onto very deep, personal feelings, moved, upset.

I have found that doing "Edith Stein" goes from being a theatrical experience to a community experience. People come back, want to discuss the issues, relate their own Holocaust experiences. Therefore, as a service to the community, it is essential that the community be allowed to speak. Every time the play has been produced so far the theater has organized a panel discussion after the matinee. Participants have included Rabbis, Priests, Survivors, and others. Universities and grade schools have brought bus loads of students. The play is topical, controversial. Do not fear. Edith brings out the wisdom in people.

Arthur Giron

COSTUME PLOT

The habits worn by Carmelite nuns are unique to that order: dark brown, a rope-like belt, a panel over the dress down the front and back—similar to the robes monks wear. Carmelites strive to keep their hands hidden underneath the front panel. The head is covered by an off-white hood that also covers the neck; on top of this is a black veil held to the hood with straight pins. Edith wears a white veil in the second act because she has not taken her final vows. Carmelites wear rope sandals.

ACT I

Prologue

Prioress
> The same Carmelite garb as the other nuns. The only difference is a wooden clapper that hangs from her waist.

Weismann
> Suit

Edith
> A simple blouse with long sleeves
> A simple skirt
> Dark stockings
> Conservative shoes that can be easily removed in Scene 2

Scene 1

Characters in the Purim play

Homemade biblical attire that covers the body completely, since these characters are actually played by actors whom we'll see later portray nuns and Nazis, but who are now members of Edith's family and friends. They also wear full or half masks, false beards, headdresses, etc.

Frau Stein
Conservative, floor-length dress, high collar, aristocratic, authoritarian

Clara
Party dress

Scene 2

Hannah
Colorful peasant-style sunny blouse and skirt
Apron
Bare feet

Old Peasant Woman (Played by Sister Prudence)
Large shawl that covers head and shoulders
Peasant outfit

Scene 3

Karl-Heinz
Floor-length Christ-like white muslin robe
Wig of long, beautiful brown hair
Matching false beard
Bare feet

Franzy
Leather jacket

Hat

Scene 4

Clara
  Teen-ager outfit, possibly a blouse, skirt, sweater, anklets

Edith
  Conservative travelling suit
  Hat
  Gloves

Scene 5

All same as before

Scene 6

Karl-Heinz
  Simple black priest's cassock, worn over Nazi shirt, dark trousers
  Black boots

Franzy
  Nazi uniform with swastika arm band

Scene 7

Edith
  Sweater
  Simple blouse and skirt

Frau Stein
  Shawl

Walking stick

Scene 8

Edith
Slip, under her blouse and skirt
Beautiful wedding gown
Wedding ring

Karl-Heinz
Dress uniform

Franzy
Dress uniform

Soldiers
Uniforms

ACT II

Scene 1
Same as before

Scene 2

Nuns
Same as before

Edith
Carmelite habit
White veil
Wedding ring

Scene 3

Karl-Heinz

Nazi uniform
Black gloves
Hat

Scene 4

Hannah
  Shabby coat

Scene 5

Franzy
  Uniform

Nazi Soldier
  Uniform

Scene 6

  Same as before

Scene 7

  Same as before

Scene 8

  Same as before

  Scene 9

  Same as before

Scene 10

Men
   In shirtsleeves
   Uniform trousers

Scene 11

Nuns
   Same, add aprons

Edith
   Same, no apron

Scene 12

Karl-Heinz
   Full dress uniform
   Long, black cape
   Black gloves
   Hat

Sister Ruth
   Same, no apron

Edith
   Same
   An undershift with a Star of David sewn over the heart

Scene 13

Edith
  Same
  Bare feet
  Tattoo on upper arms: number 44074

Women (Played by other women in the cast, including
    Clara. Shouldn't be recognizable)

  Shifts
  Gauzy, torn fabric that covers heads, faces, torsos
  Bare feet

Two Guards
  Gas masks

PERSONAL PROPERTY PLOT

(All properties should be carried on.)

ACT I

Prologue

Weismann
  Briefcase

Edith
  Cigarette
  Matches
  Pen
  Manuscript of family history

Scene 1

Edith
  Noisemakers
  Chalk
  Toy trumpet
  Scripts of the Purim play
  A large, cardboard ear

(Although the above items are handled by Edith, they should be brought on stage by another actor in a basket.)

  Cigarette
  Small suitcase

Scene 2

Edith

Same small suitcase, inside is:
Braided Challah bread

Prioress
Wooden box, inside are:
Old postcard stained with mud and blood
Old photographs
Manuscript of Edith's family history

Old Peasant Woman
(Played by actress who plays Sister Prudence.)
Basket

Hannah
Old postcard stained with mud and blood

Scene 3

Franzy
Pocket mirror
Sheet of official paper
A swastika arm band, in his pocket

Scene 4

Edith
Same small suitcase, inside is:
A box of paints

Scene 5

Edith
Same small suitcase

Sister Ruth

Small stool, for Sister Prudence

Sister Prudence
Sewing materials

Scene 6

None

Scene 7

Edith
Manuscript of family history
Suitcase
Basket, in it are:
Medal of Valor—gold with a red cross in its center,
hung on a red sash
Old clothes

(Pre-set: Two wooden boxes, many books, a samovar,
cups.)

Scene 8

Nuns
Tall candles

Prioress
Simple wooden cross

Franzy
Large, medieval sword

ACT II

Scene 1

  None

Scene 2

Edith
  An envelope
  Small stool
  Small prayer book

Scene 3

  None

Scene 4

Hannah
  Bouquet of yellow flowers

Scene 5

  None

Scene 6

Prioress
  A telegram

Scene 7

  None

Scene 8

None

Scene 9

Edith
Manuscript of family history

Scene 10

Nazi Soldier
A box containing religious objects, particularly a large rosary

Scene 11

Nuns
Pails
Soap
Brushes
Wash cloths
Brooms

Scene 12

Karl-Heinz
Envelope and letter from the Pope

Prioress
Bowl
White cloth

Edith
  Identity card

Scene 13

Edith
  Bread
  Bowl and ladle

Prioress
  Package of food wrapped in brown paper

Other Publications for Your Interest

AGNES OF GOD

(LITTLE THEATRE—DRAMA)

By JOHN PIELMEIER

3 women—1 set (bare stage)

Doctor Martha Livingstone, a court-appointed psychiatrist, is asked to determine the sanity of a young nun accused of murdering her own baby. Mother Miriam Ruth, the nun's superior, seems bent on protecting Sister Agnes from the doctor, and Livingstone's suspicions are immediately aroused. In searching for solutions to various mysteries (who killed the baby? Who fathered the child?) Livingstone forces all three women, herself included, to face some harsh realities in their own lives, and to re-examine the meaning of faith and the commitment of love. "Riveting, powerful, electrifying new drama ... three of the most magnificent performances you will see this year on any stage anywhere ... the dialogue crackles."—Rex Reed, N.Y. Daily News. "... outstanding play ... deals intelligently with questions of religion and psychology."—Mel Gussow, N.Y. Times. "... unquestionably blindingly theatrical ... cleverly executed blood and guts evening in the theatre ... three sensationally powered performances calculated to wring your withers."—Clive Barnes, N.Y. Post.   (#236)

COME BACK TO THE 5 & DIME, JIMMY DEAN, JIMMY DEAN

(ADVANCED GROUPS—DRAMA)

By ED GRACZYK

1 man, 8 women—Interior

In a small-town dime store in West Texas, the Disciples of James Dean gather for their twentieth reunion. Now a gaggle of middle-aged women, the Disciples were teenagers when Dean filmed "Giant" two decades ago in nearby Marfa. One of them, an extra in the film, has a child whom she says was conceived by Dean on the "Giant" set; the child is the Jimmy Dean of the title. The ladies' reminiscences mingle with flash-backs to their youth; then the arrival of a stunning and momentarily unrecognized woman sets off a series of confrontations that upset their self-deceptions and expose their well-hidden disappointments. "Full of homespun humor ... surefire comic gems."—N.Y. Post. "Captures convincingly the atmosphere of the 1950s."—Women's Wear Daily.   (#5147)

Other Publications for Your Interest

I'M NOT RAPPAPORT
(LITTLE THEATRE—COMEDY)

By HERB GARDNER

5 men, 2 women—Exterior

Just when we thought there would never be another joyous, laugh-filled evening on Broadway, along came this delightful play to restore our faith in the Great White Way. If you thought *A Thousand Clowns* was wonderful, wait til you take a look at *I'm Not Rappaport!* Set in a secluded spot in New York's Central Park, the play is about two octogenarians determined to fight off all attempts to put them out to pasture. Talk about an odd couple! Nat is a lifelong radical determined to fight injustice (real or imagined) who is also something of a spinner of fantasies. He has a delightful repertoire of eccentric personas, which makes the role an actor's dream. The other half of this unlikely partnership is Midge, a Black apartment super who spends his days in the park hiding out from tenants, who want him to retire. "Rambunctiously funny."—N.Y. Post. "A warm and entertaining evening."—W.W. Daily. **Tony Award Winner, Best Play 1986. Posters.**

(#11071)

CROSSING DELANCEY
(LITTLE THEATRE—COMEDY)

By SUSAN SANDLER

2 men, 3 women—Comb. Interior/Exterior.

Isabel is a young Jewish woman who lives alone and works in a NYC bookshop. When she is not pining after a handsome author who is one of her best customers, she is visiting her grandmother—who lives by herself in the "old neighborhood", Manhattan's Lower East Side. Isabel is in no hurry to get married, which worries her grandmother. The delightfully nosey old lady hires an old friend who is—can you believe this in the 1980's?—a matchmaker. Bubbie and the matchmaker come up with a Good Catch for their Isabel—Sam, a young pickle vendor. Same is no *schlemiel*, though. He likes Isabel; but he knows he is going to have to woo her, which he proceeds to do. When Isabel realizes what a cad the author is, and what a really nice man Sam is, she begins to respond; and the end of the play is really a beginning, ripe with possibilities for Isabel and "An amusing interlude for theatregoers who may have thought that simple romance and sentimentality had long since been relegated to television sitcoms...tells its unpretentious story believeably, rarely trying to make its gag lines, of which there are many, upstage its narration or outshine its heart."—N.Y. Times. "A warm and loving drama...a welcome addition to the growing body of Jewish dramatic work in this country."—Jewish Post and Opinion.

(#5739)

SHADOWLANDS
by William Nicholson

(**Little Theatre.**) **Drama.** 6m., 2f., 1 m. child. Various Ints. & Exts. Simply suggested (may be unit set). This long-running, award-winning West End and Broadway hit drama is the moving love story of C.S. Lewis, Oxford don and world-renowned author of *The Chronicles of Narnia* and *The Screwtape Letters*, and an American poet named Joy Davidman. When we first meet "Jack" Lewis, he is a confirmed bachelor in his fifties, firm in his convictions about God and about His plan for the world. To answer those doubters who persist in asking why a loving God could allow such suffering, Lewis blithely states that "Pain is God's megaphone to rouse a deaf world." Easy enough for him to say; for he himself has never felt real pain. And then, he is surprised by Joy, an American poet, married, with a young son. She and Lewis have been corresponding, but have never met until Joy comes to Britain for a visit. Jack ordinarily feels rather uncomfortable around women; but nonetheless he and Joy become fast friends. It is clear that Joy loves Jack, and he loves her; but only Joy is capable of understanding the depth and power of this emotion. Later, when she gets a divorce from her alcoholic, womanizing husband, she moves to Oxford to be near Jack, and the bewildered Lewis, theoretician of love in the abstract, finally confronts its direct presence in his own life. Grudgingly, though. He marries Joy, but only so that she can stay in the country. And then, God's megaphone finally rouses Jack. Joy, we learn, has advanced, inoperable, cancer. As he nurses her through the downhill debilitations of her illness, Jack finally realizes the transforming, awe-inspiring power of deep love between a man and a woman. "Engrossing, entertaining . . . literate, well-crafted and discreetly brilliant."—N.Y. Post. "A welcome addition to Broadway. I loved it."—WNBC-TV. "Poignant, powerful, intelligent theatre, witty and extraordinarily written."—WABC-TV. Winner, 1990 London Evening Standard Award, Best New Play.   (#21105)

THE PETITION
by Brian Clark

(**Little Theatre.**) **Drama.** 1m., 1f. Comb. Int. Hume Cronyn and Jessica starred on Broadway in this insightful new play by the author of *Who's Life is it Anyway?* playing an elderly English couple with utterly diametrically opposed political points of view. "After fifty years of marriage, Gen. Sir Edmund Milne, British Army, retired, and his wife, Elizabeth, are faced not only with divergent political stands (she has signed a petition against use of the H-bomb, he is shocked at her anti-establishment action) but with the suddenly revealed existence of the wife's terminal illness ... They are compelled to resolve the "lukewarm war" that has been waged between them, a war, as Edmund describes it, that is marked by sniper fire and random casualties. Points of view, angers and passions never spoken are aired, and Clark has his two characters reveal the stuff of two well-lived lives with charm, sharp wit and surges of emotional strength."—W.W. Daily. "Entertaining new play ... there is a melancholy sweetness—the kind of sweetness that many found in *On Golden Pond*—and yet even in the play's final gesture that sweetness never cloys, but remains spring-fresh on the palate."—N.Y. Post.   (#17970)

THE NORMAL HEART

(Advanced Groups.) **Drama.** Larry Kramer. 8m., 1f. Unit set. The New York Shakespeare Festival had quite a success with this searing drama about public and private indifference to the Acquired Immune Deficiency Syndrome plague, commonly called AIDS, and about one man's lonely fight to wake the world up to the crisis. The play has subsequently been produced to great acclaim in London and Los Angeles. Brad Davis originated the role of Ned Weeks, a gay activist enraged at the foot-dragging of both elected public officials and the gay community itself regarding AIDS. Ned not only is trying to save the world from itself, he also must confront the personal toll of AIDS when his lover contracts the disease and ultimately dies. This is more than just a gay play about a gay issue. This is a public health issue which affects all of us. He further uses this theatrical platform to plead with gay brethren to stop thinking of themselves only in terms of their sexuality, and that rampant sexual promiscuity will not only almost guarantee that they will contract AIDS; it is also bad for them as human beings. "An angry, unremitting and gripping piece of political theatre."—N.Y. Daily News. "Like the best social playwright, Kramer produces a cross-fire of life and death energies that illuminate the many issues and create a fierce and moving human drama."—Newsweek.

(#788)

A QUIET END

(Adult Groups.) **Drama.** Robin Swados. 5m. Int. Three men—a schoolteacher, an aspiring jazz pianist and an unemployed actor—have been placed in a run-down Manhattan apartment. All have lost their jobs, all have been shunned by their families, and all have AIDS. They have little in common, it seems, apart from their slowing evolving, albeit uneasy, friendships with each other, and their own mortality. The interaction of the men with a psychiatrist (heard but not seen throughout the course of the play) and the entrance into this arena of the ex-lover of one of the three—seemingly healthy, yet unsure of his future—opens up the play's true concerns: the meaning of friendship, loyalty and love. By celebrating the lives of four men who, in the face of death, become more fearlessly life-embracing instead of choosing the easier path to a quiet end, the play explores the human side of the AIDS crisis, examining how we choose to lead our lives—and how we choose to end them. "The play, as quiet in its message as in its ending, gets the measure of pain and love in a bitter-chill climate."—N.Y. Post. "In a situation that will be recognizable to most gay people, it is the chosen family rather than the biological family, that has become important to these men. Robin Swados has made an impressive debut with *A Quiet End* by accurately representing the touching relationships in such a group."—N.Y. Native.   Music Note: Samuel French, Inc. can supply a cassette tape of music from the original New York production, composed by Robin Swados, upon receipt of a refundable deposit of $25.00, (tape must be returned within one week from the close of your production) and a rental fee of $15.00 **per performance.** Use of this music in productions is **optional.**   **(#19017)**

Other Publications for Your Interest

BENEFACTORS
(LITTLE THEATRE—COMIC DRAMA)

By MICHAEL FRAYN

2 men, 2 women—Interior

Do not expect another *Noises Off*; here the multi-talented Mr. Frayn has more on his mind than Just Plain Fun. *Benefactors*, a long-running Broadway and London hit, is about doing good and do-gooding (not the same) and about the way the world changes outside your control just when you are trying to change it yourself. The story concerns an architect who has the sixties notion that if you give people good environments they will be good people. But, given a South London development to design, he is forced by town planners to go for a high-rise, characterless scheme. No sooner does he begin to believe in this scheme than the fashion for high rises goes bust. ". . . one of the subtlest plays Broadway has seen in years, by one of the most extraordinary writers of the English-speaking theater . . . more political than most political plays, more intimate than most intimate plays and wiser than almost any play around today."—Newsweek. ". . . a fine . . . very good play . . . A Christmas present for theatergoers."—WABC-TV. ". . . a high point of the theater season . . . rare wit and intelligence."—Wall Street Journal. ". . . fascinating and astonishing play . . ."—N.Y. Daily News. ". . . dazzling and devastating play . . ."—N.Y. Times. ". . . a tour de force . . . simultaneously compelling and alienating . . ."—Christian Science Monitor.   (#3980)

PACK OF LIES
(LITTLE THEATRE—DRAMA)

By HUGH WHITEMORE

3 men, 5 women—Combination interior

Bob and Barbara Jackson are a nice middle-aged English couple. Their best friends are their neighbors, Helen and Peter Kroger, who are Canadian. All is blissful in the protected, contained little world of the Jacksons; until, that is, a detective from Scotland Yard asks if his organization may use the Jackson's house as an observation station to try and foil a Soviet spy ring operating in the area. Being Good Citizens the Jacksons oblige, though they become progressively more and more put out as Scotland Yard's demands on them increase. They are really put to the test when the detective reveals to them that the spies are, in fact, their best friends the Krogers. Scotland Yard asks the Jacksons to cooperate with them to trap the spies, which really puts the Jacksons on the horns of a dilemma. Do they have the right to "betray" their friends? "This is a play about the morality of lying, not the theatrics of espionage, and, in Mr. Whitemore's view, lying is a virulent disease that saps patriots and traitors alike of their humanity."—N.Y. Times. "A crackling melodrama."—Wall St. Journal. "Absolutely engrossing . . . an evening of dynamic theatre."—N.Y. Post. "A superior British drama."—Chr. Sci. Mon.   (#18154)

Racing Demon
DAVID HARE

"Riveting."
NEW YORK MAGAZINE
"David Hare ... can shake a soul."
TIME MAGAZINE

This award-winning play premiered at the Royal National Theatre and at Lincoln Center. Attracting unwanted publicity, the Church of England is racked with dissention over matters of doctrine and practice and is at odds with the government. Reverend Lionel Espy and his team of clery struggle within this volatile climate to make sense of their mission in South London. Winner of four prestigious "Best Play" awards. 8 m., 3 f. (#19956)

Sacrilege
DIANE SHAFFER

"A play charged with genuine ideas."
WCBS TELEVISION
"Compelling. SACRILEGE moved me to tears."
VARIETY

Ellen Burstyn starred on Broadway in this riveting drama about a devout Catholic nun who is fighting the Vatican to allow women in the priesthood. Her evenutal expulsion from her order forces others to re-examine the meaning of faith, spiritual violence and the redeeming grace of God. 6 m., 3 f. (#20977)

Samuel French, Inc.
SERVING THE THEATRICAL COMMUNITY SINCE 1830